BATTLE READY

BATTLE READY

STAND
FIRM
IN
PRAYER

SUMMER LITTLE

Cover design by Joe DeLeon of DeLeon Design
Interior design by Will Rainier

International Standard Book Number: 979-8-9894441-6-8
Ebook ISBN: 979-8-9894441-7-5

Printed in the United States of America

My house will be called
a house of prayer.

—Matthew 21:13, NIV

I dedicate this book to my husband and children. Matt, I couldn't and wouldn't do this life without you. I'm eternally thankful God made me yours. Dillon, Collin, and Walker, run hard after Jesus, for He is the only One who will never fail you. Make our ceiling your floor, and go boldly before the throne and take your places. Stand firm.

CONTENTS

ACKNOWLEDGMENTS

*T*HIS BOOK IS about prayer and my journey to figuring it out for myself. I would like to thank all the pivotal people along my journey. First up is my husband, Matt. You are my oak. You are such a mighty man of God. Together we have laughed, cried, grown up, failed, gotten knocked down, and helped each other up again. You are the one who saw what was in me when I didn't know how to pray. You trusted me to parent our children, believing in who I could be. You have watched me seek God and given me wings to fly. Words will never be enough to describe what you mean to me.

Next up is my mom, April. She is a mighty woman of God and a prayer warrior. She gives the best momma hugs and loves with her whole heart even when she isn't loved in return. She introduced me to her Jesus.

My Big Pop was the patriarch of our family. He was a pastor who loved God his whole life. Had I not seen his faith through prayer as a child, I wouldn't have believed in it for myself. His move to heaven spurred the rest of us to reach deep for our own personal relationship with Jesus.

Gram, thank you for the prayers we didn't know we needed and your consistency to rely on the Father. The enemy has tried to take you out over and over, but God isn't done with you yet, and boy, am I glad. Thank you for beginning the path toward our godly heritage.

I also acknowledge the best thing I ever did: our boys, Dillon, Collin, and Walker. It is my joy to be your mother. I see your hearts for the Lord and rejoice in thanksgiving. My bold, courageous warriors, you are called to be set apart and different, even when it isn't cool or fun. I pray you go deeper with God than I've ever been. Love Him harder and seek Him more fully. Reach further than I can ever dream. You are so deeply loved. My ceiling is your floor. Keep God first; seek His voice in every decision. Grow in the Lord daily. Love hard. Be bold. Stay fierce. Stand firm.

Finally, I am thankful for friends who supported me and believed in me when I didn't believe in myself. You asked me repeatedly, "Did you write today?" You prayed for me. You pushed me. You edited for me. You know who you are. You are my Aaron and Hur who held up my arms. This is for you. Thank you.

INTRODUCTION

Hi, I'm Summer. I'm a wife and mom. My husband and I have three boys who are halfway grown. I went from having sleepless nights to waking up and they are bigger than me. Life happened so fast. You barely get a chance to grasp one phase of life, you blink, and it all changes again. Now, my sleepless nights are way different than they used to be. They went from praying to PRAYing.

As I said, I'm a mom, but I'm not just a mom. The term *just* can make one feel small and insignificant. I say that because I don't have a theological degree and am not qualified to preach. I don't have a high-end, glass-ceiling-shattering, high-income career. I don't own a house in two countries, but my Daddy owns the cattle of a thousand hills (Ps. 50:10). Everything in all creation is His, and so am I. There is nothing that I have to be or do or have in order for my Father, the Creator of the universe, to love me and call me His own. I'm not just a mom or a daughter or a girl. I am the daughter of the Most High King of kings. I am *all* He says I am, and that is enough.

If you have ever wondered if you were worthy enough, saved enough, holy enough, or loved enough for God to want you, this is the book for you. The only "I CAN DO ALL THINGS THROUGH CHRIST WHO STRENGTHENS ME" (PHIL 4:13). thing that makes me qualified to write this is experience. I've been there, done that, lost (or outgrew) the T-shirt. I've got battle scars as vivid reminders, and I'm a better person as a result.

Once a pastor asked me what my background was, and I told him, "Jesus." He laughed and asked if I had attended seminary. Not quite. Sometimes I wish I had. But then I remember my learning came from walking through the fire with the Father. This book won't be filled with what the Bible scholars would put in a book about prayer. It is full of what the Father has asked me to share with you. My qualifications come from learning how to pray from the best teacher of all, Jesus.

Besides, "I can do all things through Christ who strengthens me" (Phil. 4:13). (And so can *you*!) This is my story—how I got here, how I learned, and what He asked me to share. It is raw, uncomfortable, and personal. I hope it changes your life as He did mine. I am still a work in progress. He isn't finished with me yet. Grab your Bible, a pen, and a highlighter because a marked-up Bible and book are the best. I want this book and your Bible to look worn when we are done. Come join me on the path to His presence. Let's do this.

1

THE HOUSE THAT BUILT ME

I GREW UP IN a typical Southern Christian home. My parents raised me in church. My grandfather, whom we called Big Pop, was a minister. He was always starting a church somewhere, and when he started a church, we were there. Many of my Sundays consisted of sitting in Sunday school with my cousins and my sister; one of my aunts would teach us. Our family was called into the ministry, and my grandfather and grandmother were church planters.

He was an incredible pastor. I remember him preaching, like it was yesterday. He was one of those guys who loved the Lord and loved the Word of God. He would get excited as he made his point. A little sweat may have rolled down his head, waiting to be wiped with a hankie. Spit possibly flew from his mouth sometimes too. You may know what I mean.

My Big Pop had a baritone voice and would sing from the pulpit sometimes. I remember him reading Bible verses and preaching, and he would just break out singing some old hymn he knew. Or he would sing the Word of God like something King David would do. He just loved Jesus like I'd never seen before or have never seen since. His way of preaching was all I knew when I was a kid; I didn't know it wasn't like the rest until I grew up. He had a unique relationship with his Abba Father, and you could see it.

My mom was his only daughter. She was sandwiched between her two brothers, and they all sang. They called themselves the Singing Kimes Family. They were the real deal, with a couple of records to prove it. A normal Sunday during my childhood would be me on the front row next to my Gram and my little sister. Big Pop would be up on stage singing with his kids. My uncles would sing and play an instrument, and my mom would sing and play the piano or organ. Sometimes my Gram would join them singing or on the piano. All of us grandkids sat in the front row and tried not to get the giggles. My Big Pop just loved to praise the Lord. I can hear him with his deep baritone voice singing the old hymn "It Is Well." His voice rings in my ears sometimes and is what helped create some deep roots because the church was literally the house that built me.

When I was around two years old, my dad's work moved us to Texas. Only our immediate family moved; the rest of the family—including Big Pop—stayed in Arkansas. It must have been hard on my mom to leave her entire family. I remember many times my mother would call my Big Pop to pray. I remember as a kid, if I got sick, I would ask my mom to call him to pray. All my youth we would call him to pray for us. I guess I thought that God heard and answered him because he was a pastor. He had his own phone line to the Lord, in my book. We also called him when we had a question about God or the Bible. Calling Big Pop to pray or ask a question about the Bible or a verse was what we did. He was our biblical search engine.

While I was in elementary school, we all lived next door to one another because my grandfather started planting churches in Texas. Most of my favorite childhood memories are from those days of riding four-wheelers and jumping on the trampoline with our cousins. My cousins, my sister, and I were even baptized in our swimming pool by my grandfather. We were a well-bonded family. When they all moved away, things were never the same again, but the roots were still there. God was a huge part of our lives, and we knew who we were.

My parents didn't let the family moving stop them. We jumped right in at a church near our home that believed the way we did. My parents joined the choir and put us in kids' church, and we kept right on going. Church was all I knew. Being a Christian was who I was. I didn't know anything different. I barely knew people who weren't like me.

In high school I was the girl who hung out with my parents while my friends were partying. I had a couple of boyfriends for a short period of time. I usually got the "You're the marrying kind" comment as they moved on to another to get what they wanted. My parents were always so welcoming to my friends, regardless of whether they were believers. My mom always had food for the whole group, even if she didn't get a thank-you. Between my sister and me, we kept her busy cooking, driving around, and on her knees. She swears she prayed all the wrong guys away. Thanks, Mom.

I spent several hard years in college just trying to find myself—trying to make sure I had the religion thing down, doing all the things I was supposed to be doing as a Christian. I was a believer in Jesus. I was a follower of Jesus. I was good. Little did I know, the next boy I dated would change me forever. He told me he was a Christian, but his actions spoke louder than his words. He was abusive, and as you can guess, my life took a wrong turn, and I was headed into a spiral I didn't see coming.

All the years I was a child growing up, my mom was praying. She taught us songs and verses. She taught us about Jesus, angels, the armor of God, and what Christianity looked like—and she prayed. All the time. I had no idea the kind of praying my mother was doing. The prayers a parent prays when their children are young are different from the prayers a parent prays when their children start driving and dating. My mom's prayers had changed. She had a connection with the Holy Spirit, and together they had my best in mind.

She was very protective, and it drove me crazy. But somehow she knew when to call me. She would call, and it would stop me from whatever I was about to do. It made me mad that she called, but she was following orders. She had a direct line to the Holy Spirit. He was telling her to pray and call me because God was in the business of saving my life and using my mom to do it.

I will never forget the day I yelled at her, "You are ruining my life!" She looked at me with firmness and said, "No, I am trying to save it, honey." In that moment, I realized her protectiveness and her praying were for my good. I will never forget that day because it changed me. Then and there, it was as if I stepped outside of what I was turning into and back into who I was supposed to become. I looked at her and said, "Whoa, it's like I just stepped out of myself." I broke down and told her the truth of what was going on. In that moment, a radical change occurred and I made a full turn around and full surrender to follow Jesus. There was no turning back.

I finally realized I needed a relationship with Jesus. Religion I had covered. But a relationship? I had no clue. I became fully devoted to building my relationship with Jesus at this point. It was time for me to do this on my own, not living out my Christian walk given to me by my parents. It was time I owned my salvation and claimed Jesus for myself. I repented of my sin, asked God for forgiveness, and asked Him to change me.

> I AM HERE TO DECLARE I AM A DAUGHTER OF THE KING BECAUSE I WAS REMINDED WHO I WAS—A CHILD OF GOD.

During this time, the Lord started showing me who I was and who I was to Him. Once I started really focusing on Him, it became easier to see what I wanted for my life and what I did not. When my vision was clear, I began to see that what God wanted for me was also what I wanted.

Thanks to the foundation of faith my parents laid my entire childhood by taking us to church, teaching us about Jesus, talking about the Bible, and teaching us songs about God and Jesus, my concrete had been poured. I had the foundation for a life of godliness. Thanks to the Holy Spirit inside my mother and her obedience to following Him, praying, and believing for me, I am here to write this book. I am here to declare I am a daughter of the King because I was reminded who I was—a child of God. All the direction toward Jesus allowed me to set my feet upon the rock. God is in me, Jesus is my Savior, and the church, my parents' training, and the Word of God are part of the house that built me.

2

LIFE HAPPENS

AFTER I TURNED my life back to Jesus, God started making His plans for me clear. It took a period of healing and finding my way with Jesus, but He never let me go. I was back home and attending church with my family when I saw a handsome man at the front of the church whom I had never seen before. I had no idea that Sunday morning was the first day of the rest of my life. When we went on our first date, he asked if he could hold my hand while he prayed over the food. I approved, took his hand, and listened to him pray over our food. I looked at him when he was done and said, "Wow. I could never pray out loud like that; it would make me so uncomfortable."

At that moment, I didn't realize I was on my last first date. Nor did I know I was marrying a man who would help me walk a journey that would make something that was "not my thing" become my "thing." Only God can take your "I will never" and make it your "I will always."

Now, don't get me wrong, I knew about prayer, I prayed, and I grew up praying before meals and before bed. I just didn't pray out loud, and that was that. I didn't realize I was making an inner vow to *never* do something. But praying out loud was something other people did. It wasn't my thing. It was one of those things that I dodged and that would cause me to go into full-body sweats from my nerves.

Little did I know the vow I had made about prayer would become a hurdle in my life. My husband and I were both raised in Christian homes and believed the same, but once we were married, real life began. Between learning how to be married and cohabitating, and balancing equal time with both sides of the family, we were off to a rocky start.

We had financial struggles and bills to pay, not to mention we were living under the same roof with another person who had different perspectives on some things. If you are married, you know what I mean. Life happened. We thought we were good to go, so we began leading a church married couples' group at our home, because, hey, we knew what we were doing; after all, we had been married for about ten seconds.

I DIDN'T KNOW WHAT WAS COMING AND JUST HOW MUCH I WAS GOING TO NEED GOD.

We went from learning how to live together to having people depend on us. Our friends who were couples began to call us when they were struggling to help them sort out their issues and pray for their needs.

But wait, I don't pray out loud. I'm not OK with that. I would go into full body sweats and think or say, "I cannot do this, Lord." So my husband did it, and I would silently agree with his prayers. As I write this, I don't even remember if I had prayer time with the Lord back then. I must not have because it doesn't stand out. I don't remember asking the Lord to help me with it or anything. I just went about my life, letting my husband pray and praying silently when I needed something. I didn't know what was on the horizon. I didn't know that my prayer life needed to change. I didn't know what was coming and just how much I was going to need God.

3

THE FEAR OF THE LORD ISN'T FEAR

*B*EING RAISED IN church and in a Christian home didn't set me up for a perfect life full of only blessings and no pain. It just gave me hope in the midst of all the struggle. What I didn't realize is that all the rules of what a Christian should look like had led me to a religion rather than a relationship with Jesus. I was afraid of God. I was afraid to mess up. I was a rule follower. The moment I broke a law, I thought I was doomed.

In college I was a good girl, compared with most. I never went completely over the edge because I "knew better." Did I screw up? Yeah. The problem with me screwing up was that I was afraid to because I was taught not to. But I knew if I made mistakes, I could ask for forgiveness and change my ways. I knew better than to do something "wrong," but that doesn't always stop our free will.

I knew I didn't want God upset with me. But mostly, I didn't want to upset my parents, who had raised me right. I also didn't want to have to tell them. Admitting failure is so much worse than the punishment. I could live with a spanking, being grounded, losing my car, and other consequences. But losing their trust—that was a consequence I just couldn't handle. Living with guilt was way better than admitting failure. So if I messed up, I'd ask for forgiveness or just will it away. But that didn't work either.

I tried so hard to be a Goody Two-shoes because I had a

good reputation and so did my family and our name. I also didn't want to have my screwups displayed for all to see. I'm sure right now you're asking yourself, "What in the world is she talking about?"

Well, what I didn't know *then* but know now is I had an unhealthy fear of God. I was afraid to do wrong. I was afraid I would miss heaven. I was striving for His love instead of realizing it was there no matter what. I believe I was afraid to make another mistake. I was afraid God would play a video of my life in heaven for all to see.

This "fear" kept me on a proper path during high school. But it had a way of making me think I was better than others because I didn't do certain things. I remember judging them based on their wild ways, but I don't remember praying for God to grab hold of them and save their souls. That is not the way I thought. I was more worried about myself and doing right and looking holy.

As I got older and the pressures mounted, my wrong thinking of God got worse. I was stressing out, thinking one day everyone would see everything I have done wrong. As I said, I thought there would be a video of my life on display at heaven's gate. We would watch it, and everyone in line would see it. I would stand there and hope I would make it in. Insane, I know.

This is how I grew up. Afraid to screw up. Afraid of sin. Afraid of someone being ashamed of me. Afraid of God. I lived with this fear that when I screwed up, it would go on my record. I tried so hard not to do anything wrong, but I still did. I was living in fear. I was bringing undue shame upon myself. It was a never-ending cycle.

One day it finally came to a head. In my mind I had screwed up to the point I didn't think I could be forgiven. Based on what I knew, I was not on track for heaven either. I had such a heavy weight on my shoulders that I just couldn't bear it anymore. My mind was on repeat: "If anyone knew this about me, they would never talk to me again." Do you know this feeling? Are you afraid you've done the unforgivable? Do you live with fear of failure?

If you answered yes to any of these questions, let me shed some light on it for you—Jesus.

He is the light on that subject. He is the One who can take that thought and pain away. He is the One who can forgive you for whatever it is. He is the One who can handle it. If this is you, the *only* answer is Jesus.

Put this book down and go spend some time with Him and pray. Ask for forgiveness. Ask God to help you forgive whoever hurt you. Forgive yourself for being human and messing up. Thank Him for dying for you and loving you in spite of your sins, failures, and mistakes. Remember, "While we were still sinners, Christ died for us"

> DO YOU KNOW THIS FEELING? ARE YOU AFRAID YOU'VE DONE THE UNFORGIVABLE? DO YOU LIVE WITH FEAR OF FAILURE? IF YOU ANSWERED YES TO ANY OF THESE QUESTIONS, LET ME SHED SOME LIGHT ON IT FOR YOU—JESUS.

(Rom. 5:8). He knew you would mess up and need a savior. Lastly, let God take the pain and shame away. And this book will be here when you get back.

If you took some time for prayer, welcome back. Let's get back to the story of how I developed an unhealthy fear of God.

Where in the world had I gotten this idea of a video of my life playing in heaven to show my sin? As I write this, I think, "How ridiculous, Summer." I had no clue where this came from, so I decided to talk to my mom about it.

"Mom, I need to ask you a question. Why did you tell me

there would be a video of my life played in heaven? Where did that come from?"

"Honey," she said, "I always thought God was standing around the corner with a bat, ready to pounce if I screwed up."

"Do you still believe that?"

"Oh, heavens no. God is a just God, but He is also such a loving Father. He knows we will make mistakes; we are human. He is always ready to forgive."

Based on our conversation, my mother thought if she screwed up, God would get her. Can you imagine how afraid she was to make a mistake? This is so unhealthy, y'all. This idea of God as the "slap across the face for a mistake" is *not* who God is. Fear and punishment are not the heart of the Father, by any means. He is not a harsh God. He is a loving and forgiving God. Let me take you to where this wrong thinking came from and explain. Grab your Bible.

In the last book of the Bible, Revelation, heaven and the end of days are revealed. It's all pretty hard to understand, and I'm sure we all translate it differently. Rather than getting into a theological debate, I just want to show you the part that stumped us. This explains how I was brought up learning to fear instead of realizing it was part of God's gracious plan.

The Bible talks about the great judgment day in Revelation 20. Revelation 20:12 says, "The dead were judged according to what they had done as recorded in the books" (NIV). My mind pictured this as a video playing in heaven of all the wrongs I've done. My mom saw God with a bat. We both took it differently but literally. All our wrongs are recorded in the books. That scared me to death. I think I originally started serving God out of fear of hell. Fear Tactics to Heaven 101.

Imagine everyone standing in line, waiting to get through the pearly gates, and each one steps up to be judged. They open the Book of Life and look for your name, and then the video starts. All your failures play, and all those in line can see it. Shame begins. Then they play your good deeds and works, and all those in line can see that part too. Pride shines. Both determine your worth. One decides whether you make it in, and the other, the size of your crown and your mansion. Crazy, right? I was afraid of God because the Bible told me to fear the Lord. But that is *not* what it means.

This way of thinking is completely jacked up. This fear of doing wrong scared me, but it also kept me on the straight and narrow, for the most part. My husband was raised similarly, so for years we just followed this protocol and lived a fear-based, legalistic lifestyle, all the while not knowing this was what we were doing.

Instead of being in awe of the God of creation loving me and sending His Son for me, I was afraid of Him. The Bible says, "The fear of the LORD is the beginning of wisdom" (Prov. 9:10). Having reverence for the King of kings and His glory is where wisdom starts. This is right thinking and proper fear.

Unhealthy fear kept me striving and also enslaved. Fear is a liar. Satan twirls around like a dancer in the heart and mind by instilling fear. When life comes and you live in fear and unsure of who you are in Christ, you panic. Hard times hit, and you have to learn to survive. You can do it alone, or you can surrender to the One who takes that fear and replaces it with the faith that moves mountains.

Now we know reverence and awe is what "fear the Lord" means. Before we get into what prayer truly is further in the book, the next chapter addresses a few other foundational things that have a tendency to cause unhealthy fear. It is full of scripture and may disrupt some thinking or teaching you have learned. Take it in stride. Chew on it. Process it.

Consider the next chapter an opportunity to dig deep into your perspectives, what you have learned, and what you may not know. Some of it may shift your thinking, while some may awaken your mind to the intricacies of the Father.

Get ready. Once we tackle this, we will get into the nitty-gritty of prayer. I want to help you create a lifestyle of prayer. First, we must identify lies, see ourselves as God sees us, and finally, welcome all He has for us. It's a process, but trust me, each discovery will be worth it.

4

TWO CAUSES OF AN UNHEALTHY FEAR OF THE LORD

*T*HERE ARE TWO words—legalism and grace—that have caused confusion in Christianity. It's no secret that culture is affecting Christianity, instead of Christianity affecting culture. Sadly, these divisive words lead many people to have an unhealthy fear of God, sin, and judgment. Hopefully I can help clear it up some.

LEGALISM

Have you heard the term *legalism*? This term was not used when I was growing up. I honestly thought it was a new word, but it has been around for centuries.

Legalism is used to describe people who come across as judgmental. People who are black and white. But that is not what it means.

Legalism is based on laws, hence the root *legal*, but has nothing to do with being judgmental. It is basically a misused label that has hurt feelings and led many astray.

Legalism, also known as nomism, is described on Wikipedia as a Christian theology that is the idea that "by doing good works or by obeying the law, a person earns and merits salvation."[1] Legalism is a religious thinking that if you do good, you go to heaven. If you do good, you earn God's love. If you obey the law, Jesus will want you.

However, none of this is true. Salvation is the only way to get to heaven. The Bible says, "Believe on the Lord Jesus Christ, and you will be saved" (Acts 16:31). Jesus said Himself in John 14:6, "I am the way, the truth, and the life. No one comes to the Father except through Me." Jesus, not being a good person, saves.

Being kind, serving the poor, and doing good won't get you into heaven or loved by God. Jesus loves you because you are alive—you don't have to do anything. Remember this verse I quoted previously: Romans 5:8 says, "But God demonstrates his own love for us in this: While we were still sinners, Christ died for us" (NIV). God knows we are messed up, and He loves us anyway.

Believing in Jesus is the only way to heaven. Many religions tell you to be good and kind and love people, and you're golden. False. Choosing to believe in Jesus as your Savior is salvation. Nothing you do earns you credit or salvation. All you have to do is believe and be saved.

Salvation is the process of what Christians call being saved. When you choose to believe in and accept Jesus, you choose Him over sin and the wiles of the world. He becomes your Savior because He saves you from being a slave to sin. Salvation is a rescue mission.

Legalism originated because humans are selfish and inclined to do wrong and needed laws to keep them on the right path. This makes sense because in the beginning of the Bible in Exodus, God Himself had to set up a set of laws to help keep His people on the right path. They had a tendency to sin and fall away from Him, so He gave their leader, Moses, the Ten Commandments to help keep them in check.[2]

Clearly mankind needs a little bit of direction in order to keep their lives together. The first laws were the Ten Commandments, then a large list of laws in Exodus ranging from restitution, property laws to the sabbath, and all the ceremonial feasts. Civil and federal laws and regulations are set up and followed in each country. Even parents set up rules to keep the household running smoothly and the kids from killing each other. Laws and rules are boundaries, and we all need those.

Order and rules started at the beginning of time. Creation was done in order because God is not a God of chaos but one of order. If He had created the animals before He created land, they would've been floating in the abyss. He created each thing in order. Rules bring about order.

In the beginning, after creation, God created a special place to live called the Garden of Eden. Here, God gave mankind rules. Grab your Bible and go to Genesis 2:15–17: "The LORD God took the man and put him in the garden of Eden to till it and to keep it. And the LORD God commanded the man, saying, 'Of every tree of the garden you may freely eat, but of the tree of the knowledge of good and evil you shall not eat, for in the day that you eat from it you will surely die'" (MEV). This is the first boundary/rule in the Bible.

God walked with them in the garden and gave them all they needed, and they did exactly what God told them not to do. Blame it on the serpent, blame Eve or Adam; either way they broke the rule. Even though their punishment should've been death, God did not kill them because He is gracious and merciful. However, there was a consequence: Adam and Eve were kicked out of the garden. At the moment they took a bite, sin entered the world and disobedience became a lifestyle. So, the story begins.

Following laws is part of life. We have traffic laws we must follow, or we get a ticket. We have civil laws to keep the peace and moral laws that most follow even if they don't know God. I mean, most people don't run around killing people for fun on a daily basis. They may have no clue God asks us not to murder in the Bible, but there is something inside them that recognizes life is important.

God establishes his laws and commandments early on. Man breaks them over and over. God set up these laws with the Israelites to help them manage life outside Egypt. They had been slaves there and told what they could and couldn't do. They were told when to wake up, when to eat, when to work, and so on. Being delivered from slavery was a gift. Slavery and being told what to do was all they knew, so they quickly fell into grumbling and idolatry. God had to establish some ground rules so they would know what to do. They were a rule-following crew, and they needed new direction.

As a result, the Bible includes these laws, and they have been passed down through generations. Throughout the Bible there are rules and even suggestions as to what a Christ follower should look like. God knew we could never meet all the standards, and He never called us to be perfect. Some are suggestions to keep us safe, and some are clear commands. We all translate the Bible the way we want and argue over what is right and wrong. Some of it is pretty clear yet still questioned.

We live in a culture that claims, "Do what feels good," "You be you," and "Live your truth." In the midst of it all, the one and only truth is Jesus. God set the rules, and Jesus paid for all our sins on the cross. God knew we would break the rules. God knew we would argue over right and wrong. God knew we would defend our sin.

For these reasons we must understand the importance of the sacrifice Jesus made for us. He suffered for our sin to free us from the slavery of sin. Romans 6 talks about how we are dead to sin and alive in Christ. Once we receive salvation, we are no longer slaves to sin and its control or dominion over us. Verse 6 says, "Knowing this, that our old man has been crucified with Him, so that the body of sin might be destroyed, and we should no longer be slaves to sin" (MEV).

As believers who have chosen Jesus as our Savior; we are washed clean as a result of Jesus' death and resurrection. He set us free from the bondage of sin, and it is no longer our dictator. We choose Jesus; we choose freedom. Now our old, sinful man is gone and a new, clean slate we have been given. Will we still sin and make mistakes? Yes. But sin is no longer our ruler or our first response. Romans 6:14 says, "For sin shall not have dominion over you, for you are not under law, but under grace."

> GOD DOESN'T WANT US TO WALK AROUND AFRAID OF MAKING A MISTAKE AND AFRAID OF HIM. HE WANTS US TO FOLLOW HIM, LOVE OTHERS, AND SHARE THE GOSPEL OF HIS LOVE FOR THE WORLD.

We don't have to be like the Israelites and wander around lost, waiting on rules and a king. We have a King. Jesus gives guidelines to live by, but His mercy forgives us when we drop the ball. We can live in freedom from sin and condemnation because He paid the penalty.

Even though God knows we need direction and will make mistakes, we are forgiven because of Jesus. He was the sinless, spotless Lamb who made the sacrifice for us. Jesus was the one without sin who took our place. We don't have to earn a love of a gift that is already free. God loves you just because you're alive.

God doesn't want us to walk around afraid of making a mistake and afraid of Him. He wants us to follow Him, love others, and share the gospel of His love for the world. Being afraid of doing wrong is an unhealthy fear. We can never do enough to earn merit or favor. God knows we aren't perfect and need rules, and even so, we can't keep from breaking them.

Legalism is religious, rule following, and striving for something unachievable. Christianity is a religion based on a relationship—building a relationship with a Savior who gives us free gifts. Salvation is the first free gift (Eph. 2:8–9). This gift is followed by forgiveness, mercy, grace, love, patience, and so on. This is just the beginning of the goodness of God.

Legalism makes us fear we can never be enough even though we try. Christianity takes us as we are and leads us to become better. Striving to be good enough when we can't be is what makes many people leave the Christian life.

It took me a while to realize I had an unhealthy fear of the Lord. When the Bible says, "The fear of the Lord is the beginning of wisdom," it is talking about a reverence for God and His authority and sovereignty. He doesn't want us to be afraid of Him. God is not scary; He is loving. He wants to be our friend and Savior.

Differing opinions on the lines between right and wrong, what is and is not sin, have led to arguing and confusion. God is not the author of confusion. But the enemy loves to blur all the lines and cause confusion and division.

The Bible is pretty clear on some sin, but that doesn't mean man wants to follow what is said. But the Bible says in James 1:17, "Every good and perfect gift is from above, coming down from the Father of the heavenly lights, who does not change like shifting shadows" (NIV). In his effort to give us the best gifts and help us to a life that's less painful, God set limits and rules.

He didn't lay down ground rules to keep us from having fun. He laid down some rules to keep us from doing things that will harm us physically, emotionally, mentally, and spiritually.

He calls us to follow Him. Anyone who meets Him walks away changed. He calls us to look different and not like the unsaved world so that our lives will lead others to salvation in

Him. If we live like everyone else, how will anyone know they need Jesus to save them? If we live like everyone else, how will we bring others to Jesus?

Living differently, being set apart, means being separated from sin and alive in Christ. The purpose of salvation is to separate us from the captivity of sin. Romans 6 talks about putting away the old man who was slave to sin, and we no longer have to let sin rule our mortal bodies.

Romans 6:14 says, "For sin shall not have dominion over you." When we choose salvation through Jesus Christ, the goal is to turn from our wickedness and sin and follow Jesus. Romans 6:16 says, "To whom you yield yourselves as slaves to obey, you are slaves of the one you obey, whether of sin leading to death, or of obedience leading to righteousness."

Basically, God's kindness leads us to repentance (Rom. 2:4).

We get saved when we believe in the Lord and choose Jesus as our Savior.

Jesus asks us to turn from sin and no longer let it enslave us, and to follow Him. Following Him draws us to holiness and righteous living and away from the bondage of sin. It takes time and work, but it can be done.

Let's see what the Bible says about this subject.

Jeremiah 1:5: "Before I formed you in the womb I knew you, before you were born I set you apart; I appointed you as a prophet to the nations" (NIV).

Romans 12:2: "Do not be conformed to this world, but be transformed by the renewing of your mind, that you may prove what is that good and acceptable and perfect will of God."

1 Peter 2:9: But you are a chosen generation, a royal priesthood, a holy nation, His own special people, that you may proclaim the praises of Him who called you out of darkness into His marvelous light."

Galatians 2:20: "I have been crucified with Christ; it is no longer I who live, but Christ lives in me; and the life which I now live in the flesh I live by faith in the Son of God, who loved me and gave Himself for me."

God sent Jesus to take your sins, pay for them, and free you from the bondage of sin. He doesn't even ask anything in return. He wants us to live differently from the world to protect us from the enemy. He wants us to renew our minds in Him and His Word so we will not be swayed by the lies of the world. He wants us to be led by His Spirit instead of fleshly desires. This is not for His sake but our own. He's provided another way for you already. He took the chains of sin and death off you. All you have to do is take hold of it.

Choose to look in the mirror and see who you are through the eyes of your Savior—clean, forgiven, redeemed, set free. Let Him change your mind from following the world to following Him.

Then, you will understand the reverence and awe God alone is worthy of. Then, you will choose to live a life set apart. You will see that He loves you right now just as much as He will tomorrow, whether you screw up or not. He is worthy; you are not. But you are fully known, the best and worst of you, and fully loved.

But what if?

What if we get to heaven and a video of our life is playing (which I'm sure is not the case)? We stand there, the big book is out on the table, and the finger of God searches for your name. Jesus is standing at the right hand of the Father. He is our defender, our lawyer. Jesus is the guy who stands there, looks at God the Father, and says, "Dad, listen, yes, she was a sinner, but it's covered with My blood, and it's been taken care of. She had a debt, and I paid it. Though her sins were as scarlet, they've been washed white as snow. By My blood she's forgiven" (Isa. 1:18). The Father and Son agree. Then He turns to you and says, "We love you more than you can fathom. Well done, child. Enter into eternal life."

God agrees with Jesus because God the Father's heart for His children *is* love.

Can you picture this? It just makes my heart melt, and a smile stretches across my face. Jesus defends me to His Dad, God, the Creator of the universe. How cool is that? The Bible tells us in Romans 8:34 that Jesus is at the right hand of the Father interceding for us. Just before this part it says, "Who then will condemn us? No one" (NLT).

How beautiful is that picture? There's no striving here, just Jesus.

This is the kind of Savior I want to follow. This is the kind of person I want to draw closer to and build a relationship with. For this guy and this kind of love, I will lay down some things. I won't be perfect, but I will be fully known and fully loved. I may break a rule, but I will be forgiven. In the process of it all He will guide me to become a better person.

The law was written as boundaries. Jesus came and paid the ransom and saved us from the law we could never measure up to. Thank God for Jesus.

What does any of this have to do with prayer and your life?

Flip in your Bible to the Book of Proverbs. This book is considered the book of wisdom. Remember how the correct fear of the Lord is the beginning of wisdom. This book is your stop for finding wisdom and understanding—it has thirty-one chapters, one for each day of the month.

This book is loaded with goodness. Let's look at Proverbs 1:7: "The fear of the LORD is the beginning of knowledge, but fools despise wisdom and instruction." This one is power packed and clear.

Not only do we get wisdom from having a reverent fear of

the Lord; we also get knowledge. Part of that knowledge comes with understanding of the Lord, His ways, and His Word.

As you make your way through Proverbs, you begin to see a difference between the wise and the wicked. Some consider this the saved and unsaved. Some consider these immature and mature Christians.

In talking to many friends and collecting information for this book, I found some staggering information. Many Christians read Proverbs and find themselves in the place of the wicked. They see themselves as sinners. They see themselves as unable to meet the standards of perfection.

God does not require perfection from you! This is one of the ways legalism affects your life and your prayer life. Legalism causes you to judge others and yourself. Jesus' payment on the cross clears your debt.

Whether you have been saved thirty years or thirty minutes, your thinking can keep you from a productive Christian life and authoritative prayer life.

You have been forgiven. As a Christian, you have the choice to say the prayer once and stay in the same lifestyle—live like the world, with no differences between you and the unsaved, finding yourself stuck in your sin. This is bondage.

Taking Jesus' work on the cross and knowing you are covered under the blood of Jesus, saved, sanctified, forgiven, redeemed, and set free is your other choice. But this one may change you. You may lose your desires for sin. Your friends may change. You may gain a desire to study God's Word and want to look different from the world, begin to live set apart.

In every story in the Bible when people came across Jesus, once they met Him, they changed. Your acceptance of Jesus has the power to do just that—change you from slave to free. Who you become depends on you.

This is not a works-based change. This is part of the free gift that comes with salvation. Once you are saved, you are set free. The Bible says, "There is none righteous, no, not one" (Rom. 3:10). Jesus is the only righteous One. At the cross He replaced your sin with His righteousness, meaning you cannot earn righteousness; it was free at salvation. Your life had a stamp of sin that Jesus' blood washed off and replaced with a stamp of righteousness.

When you continue in sin, you are not fully accepting the work Jesus did for you. Meeting Jesus means change. Some get fully set free from addiction, sickness, fear, and more. Some do not. Some still struggle with addiction, but God is a God of freedom. He wants us to replace our sin and addiction with His fullness.

Full surrender to Him means being willing to change and lay some things down. Sometimes it requires a major life overhaul. Surrender may include a mind and thought reset. Surrender may require a lifestyle change. Surrender may require changing your friends or your job. Surrender is being willing to let Jesus change your life.

- Surrendering to Jesus and letting Him work in your life is where you find wholeness.
- You will no longer long for sin or the world's ways.
- You will never want to go back to where you were before.
- You will be content in who the Lord has called you to be.
- You will read Proverbs and see yourself in the wise camp.
- Jesus extracted you out of your own demise and wickedness.

- Surrender and wholeness change your prayer life.

A slave to sin will beg God to forgive you for the thing you just can't shake, or beg Him to change your spouse. A slave lives in fear and condemnation, feeling like a screwup and worried about everything. A slave feels stuck and like life is never going to change.

A slave doesn't enjoy the Bible because it doesn't make sense; it condemns. A slave prays when they need to, not because they can. A slave feels as if their friends are judgmental because they are feeling convicted. A slave defends their sin because they don't see themselves as free.

A slave is legalistic and afraid to screw up and get hit with a bat by a big God. They dwell in shame of sin they can't forgive themselves or others for. They keep sinning over and over and have half a desire to change. A slave doesn't realize they are already free. They walk around defeated, yet their victory is right there.

Now let's look at the other side of the spectrum.

A surrendered believer has peace. They read the Bible to grow deeper in love with their Savior. They understand what they read because their reverence and respect for the Lord (holy fear) have given them wisdom and knowledge. They pray with authority as a child of God. They know they are called and have a purpose. They have been given revelation as to what God says is for them and not for them. They are sold out and set free from sin. They are no longer slaves to sin but to righteousness. They walk in victory instead of defeat.

Once you surrender, you start to see things in a different light. You will still have days of doubt, but you will have learned how to turn to the Lord sooner rather than later. You will go to the throne for another dose of His presence to get you out of the funk. All this happens from having a relationship with Jesus. A desire to spend time worshipping, praying, and in His Word arises in you. When the hard times come, you will know where to go first. It is life-changing.

Reverence versus unhealthy fear is the same as surrender versus slave. They go hand in hand. Only spending time with God and allowing yourself to be vulnerable will change you from one place to the other. Spend time in worship. Spend time in His Word. Spend time in prayer. If you do these things, you will begin to see just how loved you are and change will come.

Now that you have a grasp on the purpose of laws, boundaries, and what legalism really is, let's take a look at the opposite side: grace. Grace alone is a wonderfully free gift from God that all of us get and do not deserve. Grace is unmerited favor from God. But when used incorrectly, it too can become a hazard to the Christian culture. Here we go.

LET'S TALK GRACE

One day a lady told me the Lord said to her He wanted to bless her obedience if she gave up something important. But He asked her to give up something she enjoyed. It was so important in her life that she told God she wouldn't give it up for Him. Needless to say, she gave Him the demands instead of listening to His plans for her. It had become a place of solace for her, where she went instead of to the Lord.

I am reminded of a song by Jimmy Needham called "Clear the Stage," which says that whatever comes before God is considered an idol. The entire song is spot on. We can turn so many things into idols. We don't realize what we are doing, but it gets a grip on us. Listen to the song on your favorite music streaming service.

Idols can be as simple as our figure, our hair, our car, the size of our home, a name-brand item, or even a person, an addiction, a hobby. Anything you cannot stop thinking about or doing can become an idol. When you find yourself hiding it, check yourself. When you find yourself driven by it, check yourself. When you find yourself defending it, check yourself.

It doesn't have to be bad for you to be bad for you. Too much of a good thing is still too much. Even healthy lifestyles can become idols if they take the place of God.

What does this have to do with grace?

Grace is God's unmerited favor; it is a free gift from the Lord. Without His grace we would be hopeless and without a Savior. We cannot earn it, nor do we deserve it, making it unmerited.

The Amplified Bible, Classic Edition explains Ephesians 2:8: "For it is by free grace (God's unmerited favor) that you are saved (delivered from judgment and made partakers of Christ's salvation) through [your] faith."

Most people know the verse as this: "For by grace you have been saved through faith." It's plain and simple. Basically, we have the option of salvation only because of God's grace. Then, because of our faith, we believed and chose to be saved.

Here is where the confusion lies: Just because God is generous and hands out grace doesn't mean we should abuse it.

Romans is one of the best places this is explained. Romans 5:8 tells us, "But God demonstrates His own love toward us, in that while we were still sinners, Christ died for us. Romans 5:20–22 says, "Where sin abounded, grace abounded much more, so that as sin reigned in death, even so grace might reign through righteousness to eternal life through Jesus Christ our Lord."

Previously in Romans, it was talking about how because of the sin of Adam, sin started, which led to death. "The wages of sin is death" (Rom. 6:23).

But because of the sacrifice of Jesus we are given forgiveness, grace, and eternal life when we choose salvation. "But the gift of God is eternal life in Christ Jesus our Lord." (Rom. 6:23).

Grace is one of the many free gifts that Jesus offers us, not only at salvation but when we need it. Even after salvation we will still make mistakes and sin. When we repent and ask for forgiveness, Jesus forgives us again. He does this over and over. Grace upon grace. His responses of forgiveness and grace are not our ticket to sin all we want and just claim grace as the grand prize.

Let's see what the Bible says about how God wants us to respond to grace, starting at the beginning of Romans 6.

"What shall we say then? Shall we continue in sin that grace may increase? God forbid! How shall we who died to sin live any longer in it? Do you not know that we who were baptized into Jesus Christ were baptized into His death?" (MEV).

In layman's terms, God sent Jesus to die so we could be forgiven from our sin and quit living like that. His death paid for it. Just because it is paid for doesn't mean we get a free pass to keep doing it.

Basically, "Our old man has been crucified with Him, so that the body of sin might be destroyed, and we should no longer be slaves to sin. For the one who has died is freed from sin" (Rom. 6:6–7, MEV).

Jesus won't die again. "He died to sin once for all" (Rom. 6:10). In this He set us free from being enslaved to sin. How amazing is that?

Romans 6 goes on until the end talking about you having the decision to be obedient to God and follow His path to righteousness and righteous living. Or you can remain in sin and let sin be your leader and stay obedient to sin. Again, Paul tells us, "God forbid!" (v. 15, MEV).

Romans 6:16 says that sin leads to death and obedience leads to righteousness.

But, "Thanks be to God...you have been freed from sin, you became slaves of righteousness" (Rom. 6:17–18).

Only by the grace of God did He send Jesus to die for our sins. And our belief in Him credits us with the righteousness of Jesus. We are not righteous; we are only considered righteous because of Jesus crediting us with His righteousness.

My whole point is that even though forgiveness, grace, and righteousness are free gifts from God to us, they weren't free. Jesus paid the ultimate price by sacrificing Himself for you. He covered your sin and Psalm 103:12 says, "As far as the east is from the west, so far has he removed our transgressions (sin) from us."

Jesus paid it all. Why? Because He loves you that much. And because He wants you to quit letting sin rule in your life, heart, and mind. How do I know that?

Romans 8:5: "For those who live according to the flesh set their minds on things of the flesh, but those who live according to the Spirit, set their minds on things of the Spirit."

Paul explains this in verse 6:

Carnal mind = death
Spiritual mind = life and peace

Jesus died for your sin, giving you forgiveness and grace. At salvation we get Jesus' Spirit within us. We have all we need for life and peace. But we must choose to follow the Spirit over our flesh. We have free will to choose. Which one will you obey, sin or righteousness? It's completely up to you.

The Spirit of God is alive in you and leads you toward righteous living and choosing to die to sin and the flesh. If you reject the Spirit, you will follow and obey the flesh. The choice is yours.

Some people see grace as the excuse to sin and say, "It is covered by the blood." But that is not why Jesus died. He died to free you from bondage of sin. When we get saved, we become alive in Christ. When we begin to allow His Spirit to work in us, we will not want to stay the same and let sin rule.

You have been saved by grace through your faith. Let grace lead you into the path God has designed for you that leads to freedom, righteousness, and an eternal life in Christ Jesus.

How does this work?

Move on through to Romans 12:1-2: "I urge you therefore, brothers, by the mercies of God, that you present your bodies as living sacrifices, holy and acceptable to God, which is your reasonable act of worship. Do not be conformed to the patterns of this world, but be transformed by the renewing of your mind, that you may prove what is the good, pleasing and perfect will of God."

In the Old Testament and before Jesus, the people of God had to make animal sacrifices, food and drink offerings/sacrifices to God for forgiveness. They brought them to the temple for the priest to make the sacrifices to God. Then Jesus came as the ultimate sacrifice to pay all the sin debt of the entire world.

This set of verses asks us to make our lives sacrifices to Jesus, to live lives that allow Him to transform us to live by the Spirit and not the flesh. He asks us not to look like the world. In doing this, we will be in His good, pleasing, and perfect will for our lives. Living worldly and obeying our fleshly desires is not God's best for us.

Our bodies are temples of the Holy Spirit made to worship and glorify God. First Corinthians 6:19-20 charges us, "Do you not know that your body is a temple of the Holy Spirit, who is in you, whom you have received from God, and that you are not your own? You were bought at a price. Therefore, glorify God in your body and in your spirit, which are God's."

Lastly, take a look at Titus 2:11–14: "For the grace of God that brings salvation has appeared to all men, teaching us that, denying ungodliness and worldly desires, we should live soberly, righteously, and in godliness in this present world, as we await the blessed hope and the appearing of the glory of our great God and savior Jesus Christ, who gave himself for us, that He might redeem us from all lawlessness and purify Himself a special people, zealous for good works."

Grace gives us all we need to reject worldliness and learn, as a result of the forgiveness and grace, how to represent Jesus in godliness. First Peter 1:3 explains, "His divine power has granted to us all things that pertain to life and godliness, through the knowledge of Him who called us to his own glory and excellence."

Jesus in His divine power has given us all we need. Because of the blood of Jesus and His sacrifice to cover our sins, we have access to the Holy Spirit. The Holy Spirit covers us in the righteousness of Jesus and gives us peace and the ability to trust God. All we need to do is connect more with Him and learn to walk this life in godliness. The more we pray and listen, the easier His voice and will are to understand.

Prayer is the way you connect with God. Prayer gives you a chance to lay yourself down to the Lord and ask Him to help you turn your life around. He can help if you are struggling with continual sin. He can help if you are fearful or have negative thoughts and feelings. Prayer connects us to the heart of the Father. Go to Him with your struggles, and let Him give you grace for the moment and situation. Sit back and listen and let Him guide you in all truth. The more you seek Him, the more you will find Him and the more you will begin to reflect Him.

Grace is the favor of God that we have not earned but He gave freely. Grace is meant to keep you in His will, not for you to live your way. Grace is a gift Jesus paid His life for. Represent His grace well with your life. Jesus paid it all. All to Him we owe. He sacrificed His body for you. Isn't He worthy of your life? He is!

Sometimes, in His love and grace given freely to us, God allows us to experience pain and hardship to introduce us to new measures of His love. Pain can often be a grace-filled path to a strong prayer life.

5

DEFINING MOMENTS: WHEN PRAYER BECAME ESSENTIAL

*G*RASPING THE KNOWLEDGE and understanding of God's love didn't come to me as early as I wish it had. Pain, mistakes, hard times, many falls, and many valleys led me to this truth. Even during this time, I didn't learn to pray for myself. I had my mom, my husband, and my grandparents—I didn't need to learn, or at least I didn't think I did. The problem is, I never really grasped the true concepts of God's heart of love for me until He was all I had to rely on.

I had to walk through some hard times in my life to capture who God is and who I am to Him. These moments may have been the beginning of when the Father began nudging me to a life of prayer. Here I found the understanding of Jesus as my defender.

Defining moments in my life pushed me to the point of relying on God instead of others. He used people in my life to show me how to pray. He used moments in my life to show me that I need Him and prayer is the way to get Him. To gain perspective of what makes up my story, these moments defined my journey to understanding a true attitude of prayer.

OCTOBER 2000

I was twenty-three. I had recently become pregnant, but things weren't right. My mom prayed; she cried with me; she stayed by my side. She called my Big Pop and Gram to pray because she knew I was miscarrying my first child. I didn't get it. I mean, I was a Christian, raised in a Christian home. Things

> *SATAN TOOK TWO THOUGHT PROCESSES AND WREAKED HAVOC IN MY MIND. FIRST, I WAS GOOD, AND BAD THINGS DON'T HAPPEN TO GOOD PEOPLE. SECOND, I HAD MESSED UP, AND THIS WAS GOD'S PUNISHMENT. NEITHER OF THESE ARE CORRECT THINKING.*

like this weren't supposed to happen to people like me. This day stands out to me because it was so life-altering. I thought if I was doing what I was supposed to, nothing bad would happen to me. I thought, I'm following the rules and I'm a good girl. So many questions started me on a rabbit trail.

In the back of my mind, the enemy started playing around with the fact that I had made some mistakes and this was my punishment. I had asked for forgiveness; this shouldn't be happening. I began to believe this was God getting me back. I believed this was punishment for my sin. Boy, did I have a wrong thinking of God.

Satan took two thought processes and wreaked havoc in my mind. First, I was good, and bad things don't happen to good people. Second, I had messed up, and this was God's punishment.

Neither of these are correct thinking. But in the moment, I did not realize I was so off-kilter. I had a relationship with Jesus as my Savior, but I hadn't surrendered and made Him king.

SEPTEMBER 2001

I was about eight and a half months pregnant with our first child. My house phone rang, and it was my mom on the other end. She told me to get up immediately and turn on the news. I got up, went into the living room, and turned on the television to a local news channel. I was watching and holding the phone. The World Trade Center had smoke billowing out of it.

As I watched, a plane came from behind and crashed into the second World Trade Center. I gasped, hollered for my husband, and told him what was happening. He got out of bed and ran in there to watch. What was happening? We didn't know what to think. We kept the television on, hung up with my parents, and called my in-laws to fill them in. Fear swooped in and camped out. He settled in and stayed a long time.

This was a day we will never forget. The airports closed, no planes were flying for the rest of the day, and companies and stores closed. The world stopped. We went to my in-laws' home and watched television reports all day long. We cried as we watched the city that never sleeps close down. We watched as the buildings fell and the people roamed around covered in soot, looking for someone they knew.

I will never forget the feeling I had that day. I was twenty-four and about to have my first child, and the world as I knew it would never be the same. I remember us praying as a family for our country. We were scared; we had no idea what to do. I remember being afraid to sleep and wondering if we would be bombed or destroyed in the night. I remember how the country shut down, but it also bound together. The flag began to stand for something in all our hearts. People were kind to one another but were secretly unsure. We went from believing we were safe to watching the news each day, wondering what may come next. The fear I had grown to know so well came and covered me once again.

SPRING 2002

My mother-in-law, Stevie Carol, was a woman of depth. She was so in love with Jesus and spent time with Him each day just because she liked to. She was a vibrant worshipper and couldn't care less what others thought. She was a list maker. Each day, she would write a list that looked like this:

- Coffee
- Prayer and Bible reading
- Shower, makeup, and hair
- Daily plans

Once she had her cup of coffee made, she was spending time with Jesus. My husband remembers seeing her kneeling at the couch or her bed with the Bible open each day when he was a child. I had the privilege of seeing her kneel and pray, and it was like everything around her had disappeared. Her life was a true representation of someone who spent time in the Word of God and prayer consistently. She had a heart of gold as well as a servant's heart.

After September 11 Stevie began to really feel a desire to pray for our country. She made it a point to pray for the safety of our nation, the military protecting us, and the president. She added this to her normal daily routine and would pour her heart out in prayer to the Lord for the country. She shared with me how God would lay things on her heart to pray for specifically. I had no idea what she meant at the time, but I knew it was something special between her and God.

In 2002 the family got a call that Stevie was very sick. We called a family friend who is a cardiologist at a large hospital in our area. He was able to get her in to see a specialist, who ran some tests and discovered that she had a rare autoimmune disorder called Wegener's disease. The illness hit her suddenly and took her downhill rather quickly. We went from her being normal to being hospitalized. Our oldest son, Dillon, was a baby. He was taking some of his first steps down the halls of the hospital. My husband, Matt, was at the hospital more often than I was because I wanted to keep toddler germs to a minimum. Stevie's immune system was very weakened. Before we knew it, she was knocking at heaven's door.

Matt was at the hospital while I went to church and lunch with my parents. I was standing in front of the Italian restaurant when he called from the hospital and told me she was fading. I hung up the phone and burst into tears. My parents walked out of the restaurant and saw me. I fell into my mom's arms and told her what was happening. My dad held Dillon, and my mom called out to the Lord in prayer right there on the sidewalk in front of the restaurant. I didn't even think of it then, but my mom was showing me how to go to the Lord in prayer no matter where I was. When in need, do it then and there.

While we were praying on the sidewalk, my husband, his brother, and his father were praying over Stevie in the hospital room. My husband felt as if he was supposed to pray over his mom and ask the Lord to change His mind and give us more time with her. After the prayer time they began to see a turnaround. God touched Stevie that day. The healing was not immediate, but she did get well enough to go home with medication. She had a hard road ahead. They put her on heavy medication, which caused her to lose her energy and hair. But even during this she never lost her faith that God would heal her. This faith was something that would be a big part of my lesson in learning the importance of faith and prayer.

SUMMER 2004

A few years later I was watching my mother's face distort while taking a phone call from her mother. She walked out on the balcony at the beach condo, and as I looked out, her face changed. My Gram was calling to let her know that my Big Pop, her dad, had cancer. My mom came in as white as a ghost. She just broke down as she told us the news.

My mind was in shock. I didn't understand this at all. Pastors aren't supposed to get sick. Men who serve God with their whole lives don't get the diseases of this world. My mom was not the same the rest of the trip. It was as though she knew. It was as if all the faith she always had was in question that day. No, she didn't lose her faith or stop believing God could heal, but something shifted in our whole family.

Big Pop was my go-to God guy. Everyone in the family was at a loss. None of us knew what to do with our grandfather being sick. The thought of him not being around was not on our radar. It was strange how the family wandered around not knowing what to do or where to go.

A friend suggested I call a pastor who was known for healing prayers. I figured I'd give it a shot and let this preacher who prayed powerful healing prayers pray for my grandpa. I mean, my Big Pop was the person we would call when we were sick and ask to pray for our healing. This time he was the one sick. I couldn't call him and have him pray for himself; he was already doing that. Trust me, we all were.

I gathered up the nerve to call this pastor. I spoke with him directly, and he told me that cancer was a result of having unforgiveness. He told me I needed to ask him to forgive, and I needed to go and pray over my grandfather. "Wait, what?" I asked. "You want me to pray for him? I can't do that." I went into explain mode. I told him that he was the one who prayed for us. We didn't pray for him; God heard his prayers, not mine. This dude was not understanding me here.

The pastor asked me if I was a believer, and I said, "Yes, since I was a little girl." Then he told me, "Honey, you are a child of God, just like your grandfather. God listens to the prayers of all of His children." I explained to him that I pray; I just don't pray out loud or for others out loud.

He did not respond the way I had hoped. He responded the way God meant for him to. He told me to "get over that, and go pray for your grandfather. Ask him if he has anyone he needs to forgive, and pray for God to heal him." He prayed boldness over me, and that was it. The rest was up to me. Now I had to determine if I had the nerve or the faith to do it or not.

I found the courage to ask him about any unforgiveness he had and say a little prayer for him. He was appreciative, and I was sweating through my clothes. I realized later that he wasn't holding unforgiveness; he was heartbroken. Some of the congregants from his previous church had hurt them deeply. I don't know that my Big Pop ever realized it, but the Lord showed me.

I'm not sure I believe unforgiveness causes cancer. I'm not sure why he had cancer. I'm not sure about anything, really; I just know that day was the first time I prayed out loud. It was scary, but I was in a room with people who loved and supported me, and I couldn't have been praying for a more important person to my heart. So it was worth it.

It would be a long road—my Big Pop lost his fight with cancer on March 1, 2006, but won a move to heaven with his best friend, Jesus. It was a day that changed our lives. The entire family was lost, confused, and afraid.

So many questions swirled through my head in the days and weeks to come. We didn't understand why. No one does. There are so many questions in this world that we may never understand until we reach the other side. When I had questions or needed prayer, what was I supposed to do now?

Little did we all know, our new normal would be the beginning of who God had created us to be. We were all about to step into the callings God created us for. Mine may have included prayer.

6

NOW WHAT?

*T*HE ALMIGHTY GOD was my God. I was in a relationship with Him because I followed Him and went to church and all the things Christians do. But He wasn't my best friend. He wasn't the one I turned to when I needed help. I prayed but not as I should. I had no desire to go deeper. I prayed before meals and bedtime. I read Proverbs and Psalms. I knew all the Bible stories. I knew the Lord's Prayer and had several Bible verses memorized. I mean, I was raised in church—that is what I was taught to do. And that was about as deep as it got.

I had been taught early on how to be saved and act like a Christian. My parents' religion had become my own by my choice. The difference was that I needed a deeper relationship with Jesus—not just some run-of-the-mill Christianity that took me to church on Sundays and prayed when I needed it. I wanted more.

It took me a while to conclude that I could call on Jesus myself. I could have a direct line to my heavenly Father, the way my Big Pop did. I just needed to make Him part of my life in a bigger way. I was doing all the things a Christian does; I had done quiet times before, even in high school and college. I just had never devoted myself to being consistent. I didn't have a deep personal relationship with God. I know now I needed to be spending time with Him.

I had to learn how to seek the Lord through prayer. I had to learn how to pray. I had to learn how to talk to God. I had to learn how to listen. I had to learn how to trust. Did I do everything right? Of course not. Do I now? Still no. Because of that, I know that you too can change your relationship with Jesus through your prayer life. I don't have any step-by-step process here. I do, however, have some personal stories, Bible stories, and a whole lot of what the Bible says about it in here to help.

If you are unsure about whether you can go deeper, keep reading. If you are afraid you aren't worthy, stop believing a lie. I sin every single day. I am a sinner saved by God's grace. He gives me a second chance every day and every time I need one. I am a humble daughter who is grateful to have a loving, caring Daddy who forgives me and loves me in every moment.

> WHEN HE LOOKS AT US, HE DOES NOT SEE OUR SIN AND SHAME. HE SEES HIS BLOOD THAT HAS COVERED IT ALL.

I have a Father who had to teach me to seek Him.

I had to learn how to read the Bible and not fall asleep.

I had to learn how to pray.

I had to learn that He is there anytime, anywhere, ready to listen.

I had to learn everything. Just me and Jesus.

If I can do it, you can too because God feels the same about you as He does about me. When He looks at us, He does not see our sin and shame. He sees His blood that has covered it all. He sees your sins as scarlet turned white as snow. He sees us through the lens of His righteousness. That is something to be excited about.

Join me on a journey that will change your life.

Let's get started.

7

WHAT IS PRAYER?

WHAT IS PRAYER? Prayer is basically talking to God. It is our way of communication with our heavenly Father. When we pray, we connect with God and He connects with us. It is our lifeline.

Many religions are founded on a god with no power. People cry out to their gods and never get an answer or see a change. As Christians we serve a living God! We serve a God who wants to talk with us. God knows your voice. He is waiting for you to talk to Him.

I have a friend who told me she had a dream that Jesus was sitting on her couch in her living room. She asked me what that meant. I responded, "Jesus is with you everywhere you go. He sees you working at home and raising your kids. He showed you Himself sitting on your couch so that you would know He is there with you. You are not alone. He wants you to come and sit down and spend time with Him. He's watching you do life, and He wants you to do life with Him."

Picture that. God wants to do life with you!

Prayer is your way to connect with God and let Him do life with you. He is sitting there, waiting for you to share your life with Him.

Let me connect this in your brain.

Imagine a child who goes and sits at her desk in her classroom. The room is silent. The teacher stands up in front of the class and points at the board. The daily lesson is on the board, and the kids begin working. No one speaks. The room is silent.

The kids are silent. (It's a vision, not reality.) No one ever speaks. Do the students even know each other's names? Are any of them friends? Can you imagine how odd and uncomfortable this classroom would feel?

Imagine coming home to a parent or spouse who never speaks to you. That's not a family or a marriage. You cannot build a relationship if you don't get to know each other. If you don't speak in some way, how could you ever learn from them? How could you ever fall in love and build a life? How could you teach? Words are the keys to opening the door to communication and conversation in all relationships.

Have you ever thought about how humans are the only species given a voice? Even though some people are born mute and cannot speak, or deaf and cannot hear, they are still able to communicate through sign language. We all communicate in some way or another. It is how we work. It is a desire for us to share and enjoy one another.

We all want to know someone and be known.

We search for friends who have things in common and a spouse who likes what we like. It is part of our DNA to connect to others.

Maybe God created us with this desire to connect so we could fulfill His desire to connect with us.

Genesis 1 talks about the creation of the world by God in seven days.

Do you know what one thing God did every single day? He spoke.

He spoke the world into existence. He communicated what He wanted done, and when He spoke, it happened. God created male and female in His image (Gen. 1:27). He created us to be like Him, in His image, to live in communion with Him.

In the Garden of Eden, God walked alongside Adam and Eve. They were in fellowship with one another. Have you ever gone to the park with a friend or on a date and just walked around, talking, getting to know each other? That is what it was like in the Garden of Eden. God walked around with Adam and Eve and communicated. They did life together. They walked and talked; they named the animals. Adam and Eve were in a personal relationship with God. This is what we have with God when we pray. We develop a relationship with God our Creator.

Prayer is talking to God. It's as easy as that. It's like talking to your friend or your mom or your sibling. The coolest part is this relationship isn't one-sided. God listens and God speaks.

God is always listening and waiting for you to talk to Him. So why not try it? Isn't it cool to think about how easy it is to have a relationship with the Creator of the universe? All you have to do is start talking just as you would to a friend.

As we pray, our relationship with God grows and we feel closer to Him. We learn about Him and His love for us. During this time we also learn about ourselves. He shows us who we are.

Prayer is more than getting our prayer list answered. Prayer is an admission of need. Our prayers to the Lord say, "I need You. I need You to help me. I need You to heal me. I need You to protect me. I need You to forgive me." We are admitting to God that we do not want to do this alone. We need Him to walk this road with us. We need Him to do life with us.

PRAYER IS TALKING TO GOD. IT'S AS EASY AS THAT.

Our prayer time with God shouldn't only be asking and needs. We may start with that when we first come into a relationship with God because we don't know how to do it yet. But once we grow in this relationship, it will become two-sided.

One of the greatest things we can do when we learn to pray is praise God and celebrate who He is. The Bible is full of names of God that celebrate who He is.

The first name of God we find in Genesis is YHWH, or Yahweh, or LORD in all capitals. Just in Genesis, we see God as Yahweh, Elohim, El Roi, Adonai, Savior, and Redeemer, and the angel of the LORD. If we just start each prayer thanking Him for who He is, we might find all the troubles will pale in comparison to God and His love for you.

For instance, in Genesis 16 we find Hagar in the desert, begging God to save her from her mean mistress Sarai. See, Sarai was Miss Fix It, and she had heard God tell her husband, Abram, that he would be the "Father of many nations," and she was barren. So she stepped in and gave her concubine slave to lie with her husband, and the girl got pregnant. Sarai got mad at Hagar and sent her away.

Hagar runs to the wilderness, and the angel of the Lord, Yahweh, found her and told her she was pregnant with a son. The angel told her to return and submit to Sarai. Hagar called on the name of the Lord, who spoke to her and called Him El Roi, the God who sees.

Hagar experienced two forms of God here. She saw a physical representation of God in the form of an angel. Then she named God El Roi because He found her in the wilderness in her pain and misery. He saw her right where she was and met her there. That is who God is, the God who sees you right where you are and meets you there to comfort you and give you direction.

This is just one example of how we can start our prayers worshipping God for who He is. "God, thank You for caring about me so much that You see me right where I am and know how to help me. Thank You for loving me and crawling into this pit with me and helping me find a way out."

This is the God we serve—El Roi, the God who sees.

When you have kids, you learn to pray pretty quick. I remember begging God for my first son to stop crying and to sleep. I was a young, new mom and didn't have a clue. I was so tired I would cry and beg God for him to stop. His first fever freaked me out, so I called my mom. In the wee hours of the night when I couldn't call my mom, I called on Jesus because He is always awake. A few years later we were pregnant again. Because of my first miscarriage, I lived in fear of losing this baby. So I learned to pray about that—not out loud, though; that was pushing it. I learned to pray to the Lord, just me and Him.

Fear can do some pretty crazy things in your mind, especially when you are alone in the middle of the night. My husband, who was raised in a family of boys, had to walk the path with me. I don't know why women let fear grip them easier, but he was a trooper. He helped me see that I could not let fear rule my life.

My husband did not understand fear. Fear had made itself home in my mind. It was the other voice on my shoulder that made me doubt myself and God. But my husband wasn't having it. We rebuked fear, worry, and any lying spirit many times. He knew we had to get this under control.

I still have small episodes, but we made it a habit to resist fear. The Bible tells us in James 4:7, "Resist the devil and he will flee from you." I had to learn to do this on the daily. As a new wife and new mom, I had to get a grip on fear, or fear would get the grip on me. Matt was diligent to pray for me in this regard.

When our second son developed asthma when he was two, my prayer life grew a little more. When your child is struggling to breathe, you will do anything to help him. I would lie next to him and beg God to heal him. I would get frustrated when it didn't happen immediately. But I would keep praying and begging. This is when my prayers began to change a little.

I started quoting the Bible and God's promises to me and

my son. I started claiming the promises over my son and his health, saying things like, "By your stripes he is healed. He is going to live and not die and declare the works of the Lord." Later, when he was older, I heard Lisa Bevere say on a book study video, "Praying the Word of God is praying words that are already anointed."[1] Thank you, Lisa. This changed my prayer life and my life in general.

I know God's Word is true. If He said it, He meant it. So why not use it for your benefit? It is so important to hide God's Word in your heart. Grab your Bible and some note cards and start memorizing scripture.

Then, when you pray, pray God's Word and claim the promises over your life through prayer. Pray already anointed, from-the-mouth-of-God promises! (Who else wants to shout?)

I cannot even begin to count the times I have cried out to Him. I have cried out for forgiveness. I have cried out for healing for myself and my loved ones. I have cried out in frustration and anger about situations in life. I have cried out for blessings and for Him to remove what felt like a curse.

I have learned to lean on Jesus in the good times and the bad. The times I need Him are not the only times I cry out anymore. I now lean on Him every day, sometimes all day long, to get me through. Some days I need the Father to hold my hand or carry me. Sometimes I just thank Him for all He has done and is going to do. Some days I spend time with Him just to spend time with Him. Every day is different.

After years of struggle and finding strength through prayer and leaning on the Father God, I have learned that He never leaves me. All God wants is for us to give Him time. We were created to worship Him. He longs to spend time with you. He desires a relationship with you.

Whether you have been saved your entire life or for a minute, you are His. He has chosen you. He has good plans for your life. The first step you can take is to learn about prayer and begin your journey through prayer with the Father. Come along with me, and learn what the Bible says about prayer. He's waiting.

8

TEACHING AND LEARNING

WHEN MY BOYS were young, they had to be taught how to do everything. From putting on clothes to brushing their teeth, even character issues, such as being respectful and kind. You name it, they had to be taught. Children do not come out knowing how to do all those things. Parents or guardians teach us how to do things. Every day, we learn something we didn't know. It's part of the human process.

Manners are important to teach when your children are small. Manners and rules have to be taught ahead of time at home in preparation for when you go out. Those of you who have kids know that reasoning with a toddler is mind-numbing. Don't wait to start reasoning with them when you are out to eat. By this point it's too late, and the staring will start. Instead of wanting to crawl under the booth from embarrassment, teach your kids how to act before you go out.

When we would go out to eat, we had table rules for our kids that had been taught ahead of time at our own dinner table. The rules and manners had to be followed at home and when we went out to eat. Other than training manners, you will be so glad you had table time with them. Table time is key. Teaching happens here. Listening happens here. Stories happen here. Character building happens here. Every moment around the table is worth the time.

Our boys did well out in public because we prepared them at home first.

Sometimes more things are caught than taught. Children

have to be taught how to do things; you can't just expect them to know. If things are caught, then you have to teach by action. They see the way you do something, the way you respond, the way you react, and they follow it. So at some point someone taught you that. We teach our kids every day; we learn every day. Life is a lesson in and of itself.

Here is the method by which I taught my kids when it came to household chores and life skills such as making a bed, tying shoes, brushing teeth, sweeping, vacuuming, and more:

- I will show you how to do it.
- I will do it with you.
- I will watch you do it.
- You will do it alone.

Sometimes you must do one of these more than once, but eventually they learn. Practice makes us better (because really, none of us are perfect).

This book is basically that list. It is a who, what, when, where, and why of prayer, a look back at the life of Jesus, a look back through my life and a look forward into what Father God wants to do in and through you as a result of prayer.

> *LEARNING THE IMPORTANCE OF PRAYER IS ONE OF THE BEST THINGS YOU CAN DO FOR YOURSELF AND PASS DOWN TO YOUR KIDS.*

I look back on my childhood and remember many lessons my parents taught me. I am passing some down to my children. I have added to them and taken some away. In our lives we all have been taught, seen something that was caught, and been the student learning as well as the teacher. Whether you had a good example of parenting or not, it's time for you to learn so you can teach your own children.

One area we can all get better at is prayer. Each person's relationship with the Lord will look different. But they all begin by spending time with Him and learning to pray, reading, and understanding His Word. This is a teaching that will be worth your time. This is a relationship you will never want to miss out on or lose. Learning the importance of prayer is one of the best things you can do for yourself and pass down to your kids.

Our heavenly Father is our parent. We are His children, and He wants us to learn how to be connected to Him. He can fulfill all your needs and show you how to through His Word. Let's look at the best teacher ever, Jesus. The Gospels of Matthew, Mark, Luke, and John are full of His teachings. If your Bible is a red-letter edition, you can spot His teaching in red. Jesus' words, blessings, healings, parables, and prayers are in red. He teaches about prayer and shows the importance of prayer.

Jesus taught His disciples every day. Just walking around with Him they "caught" so much. Jesus was known for leaving the group before or after teaching to the crowds. After He taught, He would go away to pray. Jesus would pray for people with groups watching. He prayed for people and asked them not to tell anyone. He did many miracles and laid hands on the sick to heal them. The Bible is full of documented history notating how Jesus showed us to pray.

Jesus taught the disciples how to pray. Following Jesus and watching Him live his life, the disciples caught the importance of prayer and how to pray. Jesus was all about prayer, teaching others and being an example. Prayer is so vital to our everyday lives. Prayer is vital to our relationship with Jesus. Grab your Bible and follow along. We are about to learn how to pray from the very best teacher, Jesus.

9

HOW TO PRAY

*O*PEN YOUR BIBLE and join me.

THE LORD'S PRAYER

Now that we know why prayer is important, let's go a little deeper and see how Jesus prayed. The Bible clearly describes for us the examples of Jesus praying. Let's dive in as Jesus leads by example. The most well-known area in the Bible about prayer is found in Matthew 6. This is called the Lord's Prayer.

In some Bibles, the Lord Jesus' words are written in red. He is teaching the crowds and disciples about God through parables. The dictionary describes a parable as a short story used to teach a lesson.

In Matthew 6, Jesus speaks on prayer in verses 5–15. This is where Jesus shows us how to pray. Let's look at this together, read each section, and break it down.

We will start in Matthew 6:5–8 (NIV).

Verse 5: "When you pray, do not be like the hypocrites, for they love to pray standing in the synagogues and on the street corners to be seen by others. Truly I tell you, they have received their reward in full."

Verse 6: "But when you pray, go into your room, close the door and pray to your Father, who is unseen. Then your Father, who sees what is done in secret, will reward you."

Verse 7: "And when you pray, do not keep on babbling like pagans, for they think they will be heard because of their many words."

Verse 8: "Do not be like them, for your Father knows what you need before you ask him."

Breakdown

Verse 5: He is *not* saying you can't pray in church. He means when you pray, pray because you want to talk to Him, not because you want someone to see you praying so they will think highly of you. This is not about popularity or religion; this is about relationship. He wants to have a relationship with you through prayer.

Verse 6: Do you have to go into your room? No. Can you? Yes! If you have room and the ability to create a place to pray, go for it. Create a special room, like a "war room," to pray in. If you don't, pray anyway. You can use a chair, a couch, the floor, your bed, the table, whatever you choose. You can shut the door and be alone. You can pray in the car, the shower, or anywhere else, for that matter. The Bible tells us to "pray without ceasing" in 1 Thessalonians 5:17. Pray when you want, when you need, or where you want. Just pray.

Verse 7: Don't be like the pagans. This verse tells us not to babble on. Does this mean we have to say short prayers only? No. Are long prayers bad? No. This verse says, "Don't be like the pagans," who would pray a long list of names of their gods they worshipped, hoping they would speak the name of the god that could help them. They babbled in hopes they would get it right. This verse means pray what you need with as many words as you need, but there is no reason to repeat or talk incessantly.

If your prayer is short, such as, "Lord, protect me," that's enough. If your prayer is long and detailed, that's fine too. If you pray from a prayer list, keep praying. God hears all our prayers, short or long.

Verse 8: Our Father knows what we need before we even ask.

He knows you by name. He knows because He loves you, He sees you, He knows what you need better than you do. So if you just pray, He knows. The how, how long, or where doesn't matter to Him. He's just waiting for you to take a moment with Him and say hi.

Now that we know there isn't a proper rule, only one way to pray, let's see how Jesus tells us to pray.

This segment in Matthew 6 is well known in the church and is called the Lord's Prayer. This is the way Jesus taught His followers to pray, and it is written in red in red-line Bibles, meaning this is the words of Jesus. Let's look together at Matthew 6:9–13 (NIV), the Lord's Prayer:

Verse 9: "This, then, is how you should pray: 'Our Father in heaven, hallowed be your name.'"

Verse 10: "Your kingdom come, your will be done, on earth as it is in heaven."

Verse 11: "Give us today our daily bread."

Verse 12: "And forgive us our debts, as we also have forgiven our debtors."

Verse 13: "And lead us not into temptation, but deliver us from the evil one."

The way I learned it adds on, "For yours is the kingdom and the power and the glory forever. Amen." My NIV study Bible does not say that, but I will keep it in there for myself because that's the way I was taught this prayer and several Bible versions include this.

This is the Lord's Prayer. This is the way Jesus prayed. This is the way Jesus taught His disciples to pray and how He says to pray. Jesus has given us a blueprint of how to pray. In my Bible I have notes all over the place. This section is all marked up because my pastor spoke on this years ago. I have also studied this and felt as if it was something to share. In this breakdown, I will use some of the notes in my Bible to help you along. I have changed the words to something the Lord gave me for this book, as not to copy my pastor's words.

BREAKDOWN

Verse 9—His name: Start your prayer by calling on the name of the Lord. It doesn't matter what name of reverence you use: God, Father, Heavenly Father, Abba Father, Dad, Daddy, Jesus, Christ, Holy One, Lord, and so on. Call on His holy name, and give Him the honor, praise, and reverence He deserves.

Lift His name up first.

Be thankful for Him before you get into your list.

It's about Him, not you.

Verse 10—kingdom: The Lord has two kingdoms, here on earth and in heaven. Our job as believers is to be the heavenly kingdom here on earth, to shine His light and share His love. Just before this, in Matthew 5:14, Jesus says, "You are the light of the world." The only way people will see or get to know Jesus is through you. Do you remember the childhood song "This Little Light of Mine"? You are the light. You are the temple of Christ here on earth representing the kingdom of heaven.

First Corinthians 6:19 tells us, "Your body is the temple of the Holy Spirit." A little later, in 1 Corinthians 12:27, the Bible says, "You are the body of Christ." Each of us is part of His kingdom. We are the representation of the Father here on earth. This verse means, "Whatever your will is for earth and man, use Me to help bring the love of heaven down."

Verse 11—daily bread: This is a promise from God to provide for us. We ask Him for so much each day. But this "daily bread" is a free gift. "Feed us today, Lord." Whether it be literal food, taking care of our needs, letting us feel His love and His presence—whatever He decides, this is our gift. He promises to take care of us today.

Verse 12a—forgiveness: Don't we *all* need this? The Bible

tells us in Psalm 103:12, "As far as the east is from the west, so far has He removed our transgressions [sins] from us." Another free gift is God's forgiveness. This forgiveness took place on the cross at Calvary. When Jesus shed His blood and died for us on the cross, He took all the sins of the world upon Himself.

First John 1:9 says, "If we confess our sins, He is faithful and just to forgive us our sins and to cleanse us from all unrighteousness." All we must do to be forgiven is ask. We are forgiven. Forgiveness is God's gift to us. His grace to forgive us and forget our sin is also a gift.

Verse 12b: The next part of Matthew 6:12 says, "as we also have forgiven our debtors." Forgiving is one of the hardest things to do in life. Just as much as we need forgiveness, we need to also forgive. We get hurt and angry and feel rejected, yet we still must forgive. If God gave us forgiveness for free, could we spare some and forgive those who hurt us too? We are called to forgive. When we forgive, we are also forgiven. It's the right thing to do. It's super hard, but the Bible tells us to.

Be Forgiving = Be Forgiven

Verse 13—temptation and evil: "Lord, keep me from being tempted, and deliver me, or save me from evil." This is our plea for God to protect us. This is our plea for our eyes and ears to be kept from seeing and hearing things we shouldn't. This is our request of God to keep us and our family from harm today.

There is a children's nursery song titled "Oh, Be Careful, Little Eyes, What You See." It warns us to guard our eyes, our ears, and what we do. This part of the prayer says, "Oh, Lord, keep me out of the snare of the enemy, and keep me from being tempted. Keep me from walking into something that will lead me into evil. Keep my path straight."

Proverbs 3:6 says, "In all your ways acknowledge Him, and He will make your paths straight" (NASB). This part of the Lord's Prayer is God's promise to look out for you.

The end says, "But deliver us from the evil one." (Yes, please.) The Bible says in 1 Peter 5:8, "Your enemy the devil prowls around like a roaring lion looking for someone to devour" (NIV). Oh, no sir. This part of the Lord's Prayer covers me from this. It asks the Father to deliver me from the evil one. Keep Satan's hands off me. I'll take that all day long, every day, thank you.

My grandfather, Big Pop, used to say, "I will not be a *whom he may.*" He meant, if the devil roams around seeking *whom he may* devour, I will not be a *whom he may.* The enemy, the devil, may roam around, but he will not devour me, in the name of Jesus. Amen to that one, Big Pop. I concur.

> JESUS IS GOD'S SON, AND HE STILL NEEDED TO PRAY. JESUS NEEDED CORRESPONDENCE WITH THE FATHER, JUST AS WE DO....PRAYER IS SO IMPORTANT AND SO POWERFUL.

Jesus gave a wonderful example of how to pray in the Lord's Prayer. If you are just beginning to pray, follow this example. The best thing is Jesus is God's Son, and He still needed to pray. Jesus needed correspondence with the Father, just as we do. He needed to present His request and know God was listening. Prayer is so important and so powerful.

10

WHO CAN PRAY?

*A*NYONE CAN PRAY.

The Bible tells us to "[call] on the name of the Lord" (Rom. 10:13). This verse actually says, "Everyone who calls on the name of the Lord will be saved" (NIV). This is repeated in Joel 2:32 and Acts 2:21.

Jesus Christ is the only way to heaven. In John 14:6, Jesus says, "I am the way, the truth, and the life. No one comes to the Father except through Me." Calling on the name of the Lord will save us. This is how we find salvation. When we experience salvation, we are connected to God at that moment. He is now part of your life.

Many explain salvation as asking Jesus to live in their hearts. This can sound confusing to the non-church crowd. Sometimes the churchy terms throw people off. Salvation is just this: If you need someone to help you figure out your life, Jesus is that guy. He's like a free counselor on call 24-7.

The Bible spells out the way to be saved in Romans 10. This chapter helps walk us through salvation so you can be saved.

Romans 10:9 says, "If you confess with your mouth Jesus is Lord, and believe in your heart that God has raised Him from the dead, you will be saved" (MEV).

When this happens, our belief in Jesus gives us access to Father God through prayer. Since you are reading this, you more than likely have already called on the Lord and been saved. Congratulations! We are a family in Christ.

If you have no idea what I'm talking about or want to know how to be saved, just follow the ABCs to salvation:

A: Accept that you are a sinner in need of a savior and in need of forgiveness of sins.

B: Believe in the Lord Jesus Christ.

C: Confess with your mouth that Jesus is Lord and that God raised Him from the dead.

Once you follow the ABCs to salvation, you are saved. You can say a small prayer to begin your journey. Make it personal, but it can go something like this:

> *God, I am sorry for all the things I have done that have hurt You or been against You. I ask that You forgive me for my wrongdoing. I know that I am a sinner and need a Savior. Please forgive me. I believe in You, God. I believe in Your Son, Jesus. I believe Jesus died on the cross for me so that my sins may be forgiven. I believe Jesus is Lord. I want to make Him Lord over my life today. Thank You for forgiving me and loving me. I choose to follow You with my life starting today.*

It is as simple as that. Welcome to the family of God! You will be so glad you made the decision to follow Christ.

Now that you have been saved, you are now in a relationship with Jesus Christ, your Savior. This means He saved you from your sin controlling your life and leading you away from Him. He saved you and gave you eternal life and the opportunity of heaven with Him. This is why we call it being *saved*, because we were saved by a Savior, Jesus Christ. It also goes with the term *salvation*, which means deliverance from harm. All the churchy words—Savior, saved, and salvation—go hand in hand.

Now that we are all saved, let's chat. Do you feel life is hard or not fun sometimes? Don't we all need a little help in our daily lives? This is where prayer comes in. When we are saved, we are immediately connected with someone who is available to rescue us, help us, and spare us.

Prayer is our lifeline. Prayer is our cry for help. Prayer is our way to connect with God. Even Jesus prayed, so it must be a necessity. If Jesus, the Son of God, needed Father God's help, don't you think we do too?

Salvation allows us access to God the Father, God the Son, which is Jesus, and the Holy Spirit. The three of them are a Godhead, known as the Trinity. They are one God. The one and only God. The only living God. As believers in God we are considered Christians, followers of Christ. We can pray to God the Father through Jesus anytime we want. And the Holy Spirit is our counselor.

It's a slick deal to get three in one.

The Bible tells us in Romans 8:26 the "[Holy] Spirit helps us in our weakness. We do not know what we ought to pray for, but the Spirit himself intercedes for us" (NIV). So, even when we don't know what to pray or how to pray, the Holy Spirit is in heaven at the right hand of God the Father interceding for us. He prays for us to God.

So if you are new to being a follower of Christ, or if you are new to prayer, don't worry. God has got you covered. You pray to God or Jesus, and the Holy Spirit covers you with prayer. How cool is that!

PRAYER IS OUR LIFELINE. PRAYER IS OUR CRY FOR HELP. PRAYER IS OUR WAY TO CONNECT WITH GOD.

Before we get started, here are some names of God that will be used in this text: God will be referred to as God, Lord, Father, heavenly Father, Creator of the universe, and Daddy.

Jesus will be referred to as Jesus, Jesus Christ, and Son of God.

The Holy Spirit will be referred to as Himself or the Spirit.

If you can speak, you can pray. If you cannot speak, you can pray in your mind. Anyone can pray. The best part about choosing to be part of the family of God is that when you pray, your prayers will be heard.

11

JESUS PRAYED AS AN EXAMPLE

*J*ESUS IS OUR example of the importance of prayer. It is a necessity. We need to pray! As mentioned before, prayer is our lifeline to the Father. It is our communication with Him. Prayer must be important if Jesus, the Son of God, needed to connect with God the Father. Let's look at what Jesus did.

First, Jesus prayed as an example to His followers. He was their teacher. They called Him Rabbi, which means teacher. Jesus was of Jewish descent, and it was customary for their culture to pray at least three times a day. They would offer praise and thanks to God in the morning, afternoon, and evening. Jesus prayed for many reasons, but one of them was as an example to His disciples, to model His faith for them. Prayer was part of who He was and how He lived His life. Prayer was a lifestyle for Jesus.

One example of this is found in the first four books of the New Testament. The books of Matthew, Mark, Luke, and John are called the Gospels. It is in these four books we see the life of Jesus and His words written in red. We also find similar stories, some books with more detail than the others. These men were Jesus' disciples and walked with Him and recorded the stories of Jesus and His miracles.

The story of Jesus feeding the multitude, or five thousand, is a well-known and loved story. Told in children's churches all across the world, this story is one for the record books in the measure of Jesus performing a miracle and is found in Matthew

14, Mark 6, Luke 9, and John 6. The Gospel of Luke records the amount of food they had to disperse as five barley loaves and two fish. Jesus had the people sit down in groups of about fifty. And this was just the count of men and did not include the women and children. Jesus took the food, and here is where He worked His magic. How? It wasn't actually magic—He prayed.

PRAYER WAS PART OF WHO HE WAS AND HOW HE LIVED HIS LIFE. PRAYER WAS A LIFESTYLE FOR JESUS.

Luke 9:16 (NIV) says, "Taking the five loaves and the two fish and looking up to heaven, he gave thanks and broke them" (see also Matthew 14:19; Mark 6:41; John 6:11, NIV). The disciples passed out the food, and all ate until they were satisfied. And to top it all off, there was food left over. How cool is this story?

Jesus prayed here as an example of His faith, giving thanks to God for the food and knowing God would take care of the rest. He thanked God, He trusted Him, and He left the rest up to God. He prayed in faith that God would handle His needs and the needs of His people. Jesus didn't ask God to do it; He thanked Him for it. He believed, and it was done.

Second, Jesus prayed for His disciples and with them. As you read in the four Gospels about the disciples, you can see that some of the disciples were chosen, some saw Him and just followed Him. A few of them who were fishermen experienced His power and left everything to follow Him. I can't find a spot in the text about Jesus praying about which ones to choose. But I mean, He is Jesus. He just spoke and hung around, and they followed Him.

Once they were His disciples, He did pray for them. This is all from the red letters, meaning Jesus' own words. The following verses are from John 17 (NIV).

Verve 11: "Holy Father, protect them by the power of your

name-the name you gave me-so that they may be one as we are one."

Verse 13: Jesus asked for God to give us "the full measure of my joy."

Verse 15: Jesus asked the Father to "protect them from the evil one."

Jesus wanted His disciples, His followers, including us, to be one with the Father as He was. He wanted us to be full of joy, protected from the evil one, and sanctified in the truth of His Word. What a powerful prayer over His followers. He experienced these things because He spent time with the Father in prayer. He knew the heart of the Father and knew He could ask these things of God in prayer. Who doesn't want a Father who wants to give us these things?

If Jesus prayed these things for His disciples, as He did in John 17:11–17, we as believers can take hold of them. We can also accept them and pray over ourselves and others. Jesus prayed for others. We can follow His example by praying for the needs of others or just praying blessings over one another. Either way there is power in prayer.

Jesus was a rock star when it came to prayer. He left His glorified heavenly body and came to earth as a man. I'm sure He really saw prayer as a lifeline to the Father. This next part seems extreme. But considering He knew what was coming, He used His time wisely.

Jesus knows prayer works, so He spent an entire night in prayer. We find this event in Luke 6:12–16. He went to the mountainside to pray, and when He was done, He designated twelve of His disciples as apostles. He knew He needed to ask the Father, who was called to walk this road with Him in ministry. He had to know He heard from God on who these men were.

The definition of *apostle* is "one sent."[1] These were the men who would have close relationship with Jesus and learn how

69

to preach alongside Him. These men would also learn to walk in the authority to perform miracles, which will come in later chapters. Jesus basically ordained these men, or anointed them as priests. He chose them specifically because He knew their journey would be hard.

There are several spots in the Gospels where we find Jesus praying with His disciples. One of the most well-known times is in the Garden of Gethsemane just before Jesus was arrested to go and be crucified. This time of prayer is not found in the Book of John. The other Gospels note the event similarly. This is a time when Jesus took the disciples to pray with Him. He needed their companionship and support through prayer.

I like Mark's remembrance, found in Mark 14:32–42. Here you find Jesus with Peter, James, and John. He tells them, "My soul is deeply sorrowful unto death. Remain here and keep watch" (v. 34, MEV). Jesus goes and prays, then comes back and finds the three asleep. He remarks, "Simon [Peter], are you sleeping? Could you not keep watch one hour? Watch and pray, lest you enter into temptation. The Spirit indeed is willing, but the flesh is weak" (vv. 37–38, MEV). Jesus left again to pray and returned to them sleeping again. They didn't pray for Jesus; they slept. The next event that happens is His arrest before His crucifixion.

There are many times in life when we need to be able to count on others to pray for us and believe with us. There are times when we will have to do it alone. There will also be times someone will say, "Ill pray for you," and may never remember. If you find a praying friend, you are blessed. You can also be a praying friend.

Either way, Jesus is an example for us in prayer—which draws the conclusion that if even Jesus thought prayer was important and necessary, we should probably make prayer important in our lives.

12

WHY SHOULD WE PRAY?

*I*F THE FATHER knows what we want before we ask (Matt. 6:8), what is the purpose of prayer? Why pray if He already knows what we need?

As we discussed, prayer is our way of connecting with God. Prayer is our lifeline to the only One who can help us. Now, let's look at why it is important and necessary to pray.

Psalm 32:6 says, "Let everyone who is godly pray" (NASB). In 1 Thessalonians 5:16–18 we are told to "rejoice always, pray continually, give thanks in all circumstances; for this is God's will for you in Christ Jesus" (NIV). Several other versions, including the MEV, say, "Pray without ceasing." This does not mean we have to pray all the time and not do anything else. It just means we can be in constant contact with God. If we can learn to connect throughout our day, don't you think you would begin to see some changes in your situations?

> "REJOICE ALWAYS, PRAY CONTINUALLY, GIVE THANKS IN ALL CIRCUMSTANCES; FOR THIS IS GOD'S WILL FOR YOU IN CHRIST JESUS" (1 THESS. 5:16-18, NIV).

What if learning to talk with God as if talking to a spouse or a friend became a normal way of life for you? Do you think it would change anything? Do you think you would change? What about your perspectives? Maybe prayer is about changing your heart. Toward yourself. Toward mankind. Toward your spouse. Toward your boss. What if…? Let's see what the Bible says about prayer and why we should connect with God.

Second Chronicles 7:14 declares, "If my people, who are called by my name, will humble themselves and pray and seek my face and turn from their wicked ways, then I will hear from heaven, and I will forgive their sin and will heal their land" (NIV).

This is a whole mouthful of greatness right here! The nerd in me has to tell you this is a conditional sentence. This verse is an if-then clause. This means the condition of this happening has a consequence. Every decision has a consequence, whether it is a good one or a bad one. This verse has a consequence. If we do what it says, then there will be a consequence to our actions. Let me take you deeper into this because it's too good to keep to myself.

Humble is defined as "showing a...low estimate of one's own importance, submission."[1] Being humble doesn't mean we are not important. It means we realize life is not all about us. Sometimes I think, "The world revolves around the sun, not you." It's not *all* about you. Let's change that previous saying from you to me and sun to Son. "The world revolves around the Son, not me." This is about you and your relationship with God, taking the time to set your wants and needs aside for a moment to seek Him in prayer.

So what does 2 Chronicles tell us to do? Humble ourselves and pray. Realize it's not all about you, and pray. Just stop and give Him a moment of your time. Start by saying, "Thank You," and being appreciative for all God has given you or done for you. I can guarantee that once you've been grateful, your cry for help will be less desperate. You will recognize all God has done already and begin to know He will do it again. Your belief will grow, and your faith will increase. You will see He is a faithful and trustworthy God.

Now that you recognize His goodness, present your request to God. He is listening. He wants to have time with you. He wants us to seek His face. He wants us to run to Him—2

Chronicles 7:14 says, "Seek [Him] and turn from [our] wicked ways." God is not calling you wicked. But if you are living in sin and not serving God with your life, He wants you to stop. He wants you to take a moment to humble yourself and pray. Turn from your wicked ways and return to Him. Ask for forgiveness. Ask for help to stop and change. Once you do, the promise comes.

The next line is, "Then I will hear from heaven, and I will forgive their sin and will heal their land." Yep, I'll take that one, please—a listening God, forgiveness, and national healing. Can I get an amen? God is basically just asking for a moment of your time. He's saying, "Hey, lay everything else aside for a moment and seek Me, and you will find Me; I am ready to listen and move." When we stop and humble ourselves and pray, things change. The if-then of this verse tells us what will happen when we do. If we stop and humble ourselves, then He will…

"Then I will hear from heaven, and I will forgive their sin and will heal their land."

If we humbly pray, then God will hear us. He will forgive us. He will heal our land. Who here doesn't want to pray after hearing this promise? How cool is that? God will take time out to listen to our prayer, forgive us, and heal our land. A God who listens and responds is a God worthy of a moment of our time.

To be heard, all we have to do is pray. To be forgiven, all we have to do is pray and ask for forgiveness. To find help in our land, all we have to do is pray. This is just one verse that tells us the importance of prayer. Fellowship with God in prayer is part of our purpose as believers. You are the beacon of light to show the world Jesus. When we pray and spend time with the Lord, our light grows. When we pray, we get filled back up with our purpose. When we pray, our faith grows and we become the light the world needs.

Let's look at what the Bible says about purpose. Romans 8:28 says, "And we know that in all things God works for the good of those who love him, who have been called according to his purpose" (NIV). The passage goes on to say that we are called to be Christlike. This means to look like Christ in our words, thoughts, and actions. Then, Romans 8:31 says, "If God is for us, who can be against us?" He works things out for our good because we are His. No matter who is against us, God is on our side. If God is for me, He deserves a moment of my time.

Wrapping up the three scriptures, here is what we find: If we obey the scripture in Chronicles 2 and "humble [ourselves] and pray and seek [His] face," we are acknowledging that we know we are under God's authority and need His help. In turning from our wicked ways, we are declaring we believe His way is better than the ways of this world. If we do this, His Word promises us God "will hear from heaven...forgive [our] sin and...heal [our] land" (NIV). Praise Jesus.

One of these things is worth praying for. Pick one: God hears our prayers; our sins are forgiven; He heals our land. That's not to mention He will work things out for our good and be on our side. Either one you choose is a good bet. Guess what, we don't have to pick; He will do all of them!

If you are not sold on the importance of prayer yet, let me throw you a few more ground balls. Jeremiah is full of so many good verses, but let's jump in at Jeremiah 29. Most of you know Jeremiah 29:11: "'For I know the plans I have for you,' declares the LORD, 'plans to prosper you and not to harm you, plans to give you hope and a future'" (NIV).

I personally am so glad God has a plan for me. I do not want to go this road alone. Knowing He has a plan for my good makes me feel safe and guided. It's a "Jesus, take the wheel" kind of life. I do not want to drive myself—been there, done that, hit a curb, and wrecked the car. I want Jesus to drive this thing.

Jeremiah 29:11 is a popular verse, but most learn this one and don't go beyond it and keep reading. If you keep reading, you'll see that Jeremiah 29:12–14 is full of hidden gems.

Verse 12: "Then you will call on me and come and pray to me, and I will listen to you" (NIV).

Verse 13: "You will seek me and find me when you seek me with all your heart" (NIV).

Verse 14: "'I will be found by you,' declares the LORD, 'and will bring you back from captivity'" (NIV).

Oh my goodness, did you see that? Reread it, if you must. The Lord tells us that if we pray, He will listen. We all desire to be heard. God listens. When we pray and look for Him and desire to find Him, we will. He can be found. He is waiting for you to find Him. Not only will we find Him but He will bring us out of captivity. Captivity. We are slaves to ourselves. We allow ourselves to think bad thoughts about ourselves for making mistakes and not being perfect. We all deal with some kind of junk, or baggage, that holds us down. This is saying He will take our baggage. It's a promise! It is written in the Bible more than once.

"Cast your burden on the LORD, and He will sustain you" (Ps. 55:22, MEV). Then, 1 Peter 5:7 says, "Cast all your care (anxieties) upon Him, because He cares for you" (MEV). He is saying He will climb down in that pit you are sitting in and sit with you. He will sit until you are ready to come out, and then, guess what, He is the way out! He is the lifeline, remember. He has the rope to get you out, maybe even a ladder.

He will bring you back from captivity. Amen! You are no longer a slave to fear, rejection, shame, condemnation, bitterness, unbelief, anger, envy, self-hatred, you name it. You are no longer a captive. Our God will bring you back from your captivity!

His promise says in Matthew 11:29–30, "Take my yoke upon you and learn from me, for I am gentle and humble in heart, and you will find rest for your souls. For my yoke is easy and my burden is light" (NIV). Friends, take that heavy backpack off your shoulders and leave it in the pit. Get on that ladder with Jesus, and let Him rescue you from your pit of captivity! It's that simple.

Prayer can do this for you. Prayer allows you to find God, find yourself, and get rid of all your worries and anxieties. When you are found, He will bring you out of the depths and set you upright.

This seems like a game of hide-and-seek. God hasn't been hiding. He knew where He was all along. He also knows where you are. He has been waiting for you to find Him and give Him yourself. When you find Him and seek Him, He is waiting to give you these promises. These treasures are all yours!

You have so many gifts at your disposal just because you chose to give your life to the Lord. Now all you have to do is pray to get them. There is not another person, place, or thing in the world that can offer this kind of deal. That's not to mention how valued and full you will feel. If you will begin to set aside time to spend with the Lord in prayer, it will change your entire life. He wants to be your friend. You have the opportunity for a close relationship with the Creator of the world. He is waiting. Jump in; the water is fine. Jesus is a well that will fill you, and you will never thirst again. His well never runs dry. Taste and see, my friend. It's a wonderful life.

13

WHEN SHOULD WE PRAY?

WHEN SHOULD WE pray? People ask this question over and over. Let's look and see. The Bible talks constantly about when Jesus prayed. He prayed alone and when He was with His disciples, in front of crowds and before His meals. He prayed before He healed the sick, for the Father's help, and after He performed a miracle. He prayed for Himself. He prayed asking the Father about His will and about important decisions. Colossians 4:2 tells us to "devote [ourselves] to prayer" (NIV). Make it a habit, not a duty. Allow prayer to become something you desire to do. Jesus also taught the importance of prayer. In Matthew 21:22 Jesus says, "If you believe, you will receive whatever you ask for in prayer" (NIV). Jesus knew this promise and believed it, so He took prayer seriously. Let's look at what the Bible says about the times we can pray.

PRAY WHEN YOU DON'T KNOW WHAT TO DO

We can pray when we don't know what to do. John 5:19–20 says, "I tell you, the Son can do nothing by himself; he can do only what he sees his Father doing, because whatever the Father does the Son also does. For the Father loves the Son and shows him all he does" (NIV). Jesus went to the Father when He didn't know what to do. He went to the Father to ask for guidance and wisdom. We have the ability to do the same thing.

The Bible tells us in Proverbs 3:5–6, "Trust in the LORD with all your heart, and lean not on your own understanding; in all your ways acknowledge Him, and He shall direct your paths." We all go through times when we don't know what to do or how to handle a situation. When you learn to pray and spend time with the Lord, you begin to see He wants to be part of your life. He wants to help guide your path, show you the way.

PRAY WHEN YOU HAVE A NEED

Mark 11:22–26 spells it out for us when it says we need to "have faith in God." Verse 24 says, "Whatever you ask for in prayer, believe that you have received it, and it will be yours" (NIV). When we have a need and we pray about it, if we have faith, we shall receive it. This does not mean pray for a Ferrari and a million dollars, and they fall from heaven (not to limit God; He can do what He wants to do). But let's be realistic with our prayers of need.

> WHEN YOU LEARN TO PRAY AND SPEND TIME WITH THE LORD, YOU BEGIN TO SEE HE WANTS TO BE PART OF YOUR LIFE. HE WANTS TO HELP GUIDE YOUR PATH, SHOW YOU THE WAY.

It means that God will take care of you, heal you, and provide for your needs. Here is a promise from Philippians 4:19: "My God shall supply all [my needs] according to His riches in glory by Christ Jesus." He doesn't want you to just get by; He wants you to be taken care of.

Whether you are sick, need a job, need someone to comfort you, need a roommate, or have any other issue, He tells us that He wants to supply our needs. All we have to do is ask in faith and believe that He is willing and able, and we shall receive it.

If you are unsure if you believe He really wants to take care of you, look at Matthew 7:11: "If you, then, though you are evil, know how to give good gifts to your children, how much more will your Father in heaven give good gifts to those who ask him!" (NIV). We give our kids gifts at birthdays and Christmas to celebrate them and to show our love. If we do this, imagine how much the Lord wants to give to you.

You are His child, created in His image. He wants to show off for you. Here's how much: "Now to Him who is able to do exceedingly abundantly above all that we ask or think, according to the power that works in us, to Him be glory" (Eph. 3:20, NIV). He doesn't want to just meet your needs. He wants to give you extravagantly, exceedingly more than your mind can even dream up to ask or imagine. His love for you is extravagant. He wants to bless your socks off. This is about more than money and things; this is about abundance in Him.

PRAY TO RELAX

Another word for *relaxation* is rest. God's Word is full of promises of rest. We run at such a fast pace these days. We feel guilty if we sit down to rest. I have actually jumped out of my chair when the back door has opened unexpectedly. I was ashamed of my rest. My husband doesn't pressure me in any way; he actually laughed when I told him about this. I shame myself for stopping. We all need a break. We all need to rest ourselves. Even the Creator of the universe rested. Genesis 2:2 says, "By the seventh day God had finished the work he had been doing; so on the seventh day he rested from all his work" (NIV). He blessed this day and made it holy. We call this our Sabbath, the day of rest.

Rest is something we all need. Scientists say our bodies need at least eight hours of sleep a night to be fully rested in the morning. This is a little different from the rest you get when you spend time in prayer. Psalm 62:1–2 says, "My soul finds rest in God; my salvation comes from him. Truly he is my rock and my salvation; he is my fortress, I will never be shaken" (NIV).

Just writing this I want to jump up and down and holler. I

know it sounds crazy, but reread those verses. My soul finds rest in the God of my salvation. He is my rock and my fortress. Imagine a tall rock fortress that has a nice, comfy bed. You enter into this place and know you are safe, protected, and can sleep undisturbed, not to be shaken. This is the kind of rest you can find in the Father when you pray and spend time with Him. He is a strong, safe haven for you to go to and let your guard down. Let Him comfort you, and find His rest.

PRAY WHEN YOU ARE AFRAID

One of my favorites that I often use as a reminder is found in Philippians 4:6–7: "Do not be anxious about anything, but in every situation, by prayer and petition, with thanksgiving, present your requests to God. And the peace of God, which transcends all understanding, will guard your hearts and your minds in Christ Jesus."

Pray when you are afraid. "Whenever I am afraid, I will trust in You" (Ps. 56:3). The Lord tells us not to be anxious but to pray and thank Him for being our God who takes away our fears. When we do this, He will fill our hearts and our minds with His peace that is so incredible it is too hard for us to understand. His peace is beyond our logic.

He continues in Philippians 4 to say that we need to set our minds on good things that will help us think differently. Our thoughts affect our mood and our actions. "Whatever is true, whatever is noble, whatever is right, whatever is pure, whatever is lovely, whatever is admirable—if anything is excellent or praiseworthy—think about such things" (v. 8, NIV). If we can set our minds on good things, we can fall away from the anxiety and into His peace.

Second Timothy 1:7 reminds us, "God has not given us a spirit of fear, but of power and of love and of a sound mind." Shifting our focus to the things He wants to give us will renew our minds and lead us to peace. Isaiah 26:3 tells us, "You will keep in perfect peace those whose minds are steadfast, because they trust in you" (NIV). We can come to a place of peace.

When we spend time in prayer and time with the Lord, He shifts our thinking and our perspective. We begin to find that He is trustworthy and enjoy our time with Him. As we ask Him for things and get to know the heart of the Father, He is shifting things in our hearts to show us how to be more like Him. We can go from fearful to fearless. Speaking from experience, this is a shift worth the risk.

PRAY FOR HEALTH AND HEALING

Healing is a whole other aspect of prayer. Some believe in it, while others still wonder if God still heals. The Bible says that the Father is "the same yesterday, today, and forever" (Heb. 13:8). He is still the same God who healed the blind, lame, deaf, and mute in the Bible. He is still our Healer. His Word promises He will heal. The question is not if He will, but will you believe He can? Isaiah 53:5 says, "By His stripes we are healed." God the Father sent Jesus the Son to earth to save the lost, to be our salvation. Jesus is our bridge to God, our connection.

When Jesus died on the cross for our sins, He shed His blood for us. He was beaten and wounded and shed His blood so that we may have healing, salvation, and eternal life. Isaiah 53:5 paints us a picture: "He was wounded for our transgressions (disobedience), He was bruised for our iniquities (sins/immoral behavior); the chastisement for our peace was upon Him, and by His stripes we are healed."

Luke 9:11 tells us Jesus "healed those who had need of healing." The Gospels of Matthew 9:20, Mark 5:25, and Luke 8:43 tell the story of a woman who had a blood disease for years. She knew if she could just touch Jesus, she could be healed. She made her way to Him and touched the hem of His robe and was healed.

Jesus knew when it happened and said, "Who touched me?" (Mark 5:31; Luke 8:45). When He saw the woman come and bow down in apology, He said to her, "Daughter, your faith has healed you. Go in peace and be freed from your suffering" (Mark 5:34, NIV) You have to check this story out for yourself. She believed He could heal her, and He did. You can also be healed.

Do you have the faith to believe God can do it?

If we are truly created in His image, as Genesis 1:27 says, then we have the authority by the power invested in us by our Creator God to ask for healing. Jesus paid for all our sin and suffering on the cross. He was bruised and bled for you. He knows pain like no pain we have ever felt. He knows.

The cross has the final word. Therefore, we have the authority, given to us by the blood of Jesus, to take our sickness and pain and put it "under the blood." Declare with your mouth, "By your stripes I am healed. I lay my sickness and pain under the blood of Jesus at the foot of the cross. I am healed in the name of Jesus." Say it, then believe it.

James 5 talks about patience and prayer. James 5:15 says, "The prayer of faith will save the sick, and the Lord will raise him up." If you don't have the faith to believe for healing, ask someone who does to pray for you. Maybe after you hear them pray, you will find some faith of your own. Sometimes it takes someone else to believe for you to catch the fire of faith and believe too.

James 5 mentions some cool things about prayer, if you get a chance to check it out. Here's a quick wrap-up. Pray; sing psalms. Pray over them and anoint them with oil. Prayer of faith will raise him up. Confess your sins. Pray for one another so you may be healed. Pray earnestly; then pray again (vv. 13–18).

James 5:16 says, "The effective, fervent prayer of a righteous man accomplishes much."

Give it a try, pray about it, believe it, declare it, and see it happen for you today. If you don't see it immediately, pray again. Be patient; sometimes God answers immediately, and sometimes He doesn't. But no matter what the result, your faith will grow, and even if He doesn't heal you, He is still good and worthy of all of it.

PRAY FOR THOSE WITH WHOM YOU ARE ANGRY

My momma used to tell me, "You draw more flies with honey than you do with vinegar." It was her way of telling me to be kind. Kindness gets you further. We all know it's hard to be kind to someone who has mistreated you. In fact, be kind is the last thing we want to do. When we are mistreated, we want to retaliate. Our nature is to react. A reaction is usually full of anger, rude words, bitterness, and more. The Bible tells us how to treat our enemy, or someone who has hurt us. The Bible tells us to pray for them; it's in red, from the mouth of Jesus. Matthew 5:44 says, "Love your enemies and pray for those who persecute you" (NIV).

I have been here so many times. Pray for the people who hurt us is the last thing any of us want to do. But the Holy Spirit is good to nudge us and remind us to forgive. Ephesians 4:32 tells us, "Be kind to one another, tenderhearted, forgiving one another, even as God in Christ forgave you." A typical response to the Lord here could be: "Well, I would be kind to them if they would've been kind to me. But they hurt me, so I don't want to."

And God's response is clear in Matthew 6:14–15, where Jesus

says, "For if you forgive other people when they sin against you, your heavenly Father will also forgive you. But if you do not forgive others their sins, your Father will not forgive your sins" (NIV). Whoa. What? So if I want to be forgiven, I have to forgive others? Yes. And the best way to forgive someone is to pray for them.

How is praying for them going to help? As you pray, your heart will change toward them. No one can talk to God and pray for sickness and death over another person. That's just harsh. Even a prayer sent in anger and hurt will turn into a prayer of blessing as you speak it out to the Father. As angry and hurt as we are, the Bible tells us in Ephesians 4:26, "In your anger do not sin. Do not let the sun go down while you are still angry."

Do you really wish for awful things to come upon someone? Maybe. But do you pray for something terrible to happen to their Creator, who loves them? No. In the midst of the prayer your heart changes. James 1:19 says, "Be quick to hear, slow to speak, and slow to anger" (NASB). So as hurt as we are and as mad as they made you, we are called to forgive. We are called to pray for them and not go to bed angry.

You may say it's hard to rest and not go to sleep angry. The Lord promises us rest as well. If we find ourselves in a situation we can't handle, we should turn to Him in prayer. In Matthew 11:28–30, Jesus asks us to "come to me, all you who are weary and burdened, and I will give you rest. Take my yoke upon you and learn from me" (NIV).

We are called to pray so we can find peace in the midst of the anger and frustration. God even wants us to pray blessings over them. Romans 12:14 says to "bless those who persecute you." Really? Now we don't just have to pray for them; we have to ask God to bless them. Really? This is so hard. But when we do what the Bible tells us to, a heart change occurs. The Bible promises peace in many scriptures, but one fits this situation. John 16:33 says, "I have said these things to you, that in me you may have peace. In the world you will have tribulation. But take heart; I have overcome the world" (ESV).

Praying for others and over ourselves in a time when we have been hurt or angry is hard. Our human nature is to turn and run. It's the whole fight-or-flight scenario. We want to turn and fight and defend ourselves with cruel words. We don't want to pray for them. Or we want to flee the situation. We don't want to trust them anymore; we put up walls to prevent ourselves from being hurt again. Listen, we've all been there and will be again.

This is a lesson for all of us. God wants us to be aware that we can pray when we are angry. He knows we will get hurt and angry. He knows we will want to retaliate or run away. But God also knows that if we come to Him when we feel this way, healing can be found. He will heal our hurts and our hearts. When we pray about the situation and for the person who caused us pain, a new kind of healing occurs within us. We are now releasing control of our emotions and actions to God. Man no longer has control; God does.

PRAY WHEN YOU NEED SOMEONE TO TALK TO

God never sleeps and is always listening. When you have no one else to talk to and nowhere else to go, go to the Father. Just talk. He will listen. Eventually, you will feel better and He will bring you peace. Then, you will start to like spending time with Him and start to trust His goodness and faithfulness. When you get to know Him, He is such a great friend, full of love, compassion, and understanding.

14

WHERE CAN WE PRAY?

*T*HIS IS A fun one! The Bible gives us so many ideas of where we can pray. You don't have to have a perfect spot. You don't have to have a prayer closet, but you can. You can pray in a chair, in the car, in the shower. You can pray in bed, in the kitchen, in the bedroom, in the yard. You can pray silently in your mind, as you write. You can pray out loud or in a whisper. Anywhere you pray is OK! I have prayed in all these locations.

I remember when I was first learning to pray out loud. I started by praying when I was cleaning the house. No one was home to hear me. It was just me and God. No one was there to judge me on my words, my technique, or how it sounded. I was learning, and God was listening.

One of the times I remember praying the most was when I was sweeping the floor. I would hold that broom and go to town. I would pray the verses I knew. In a way, I was holding God's feet to the fire. I would remind Him of His promises in the Bible, as if He had forgotten. I would cry out to Him and beg Him sometimes. Other times I would just thank Him for being so good to me when I didn't deserve it. Sometimes I would be upset and not so nice. I know it was probably not the best way to go about it, but you know what? God was listening. He is tough. God can take it when we pray and aren't in a good place.

Should we pray only when we need Him? Should we pray only when we are at the end of our rope? God wants us to come to Him in every place we are in. If we pray all the time and stay in an attitude of prayer with Him, when we do need Him, we will be more powerful in our prayers. The more we pray, the better we get at it. More than that, the more we pray, the more we are in tune with the Spirit of God and His plans for us.

In writing this, I have wondered what other people do. None of us are the same; we all tend to do things differently. So I put out a question to some people I know. I asked several friends where they pray, and they all have different places they pray. Surprised? One friend prays in a chair in her room. It's her "prayer closet." She doesn't have a special room, just a chair, a spot. She may sit, she may kneel, but that is her place she spends her time with God.

Another friend prays in her car. She listens to pastor podcasts on her drive to work, and she spends her time with the Lord as she drives and sits in traffic. She has a radio to play her worship music and her podcasts. She meets with Him in the quiet driver's seat of her car. I bet she has angels all around her car.

I have another friend who prays in her closet. She hasn't removed everything; it is still her closet, but that is the place she prays. Still another friend prays in her closet, but she prays in the dark of her closet. She doesn't turn on the light, but she sits on the floor and meets with her Father in the dark, quiet of her closet.

My mother-in-law used to pray on her couch. My husband remembers her kneeling on the floor with her Bible open and her head in her arms, praying at the living room couch. He would wake up as a child and find his mom in prayer and sit and play at her feet. What a picture.

I pray washing dishes, doing laundry, in the shower and the car. I've spent many football games praying for my boys and their teammates. Most of my quiet times are at my kitchen table. I like to spread out. I like to play my worship music on my phone and sit and soak in the presence of the Lord. Sometimes I screen-mirror my phone to my television and have a mini concert in my living room as I walk from room to room and pray. We are all different. We all have our ways and our place. God doesn't care; He just wants you.

A couple of my friends have actual prayer closets. They have made rooms that are specifically for prayer. They have them decorated and have a place to sit, music to listen to. The coolest prayer closet I have ever seen has wallpaper that a wife had made special for her husband. The wallpaper is words he wrote in his journal from his prayer time. The walls of this prayer closet are covered with handwritten prayer requests, revelations from the Lord during quiet time, words and promises from the Lord, and more. It is the best I've seen because it is so personalized. This is not necessary or required, though. God wants us whenever and wherever. He just wants you!

WHAT HAPPENS WHEN WE PRAY?

I was shown how to pray when my parents prayed. We would pray before a meal, say our bedtime prayers, and pray in church. My mom would say her special armor-of-God prayer in the car on the way to school. I remember getting out of the car every day with confidence. If we had a test, we would tell her, and she would cover that too. I had no idea what the power of prayer was as a child.

Prayer was something my mom did. It was something we did before meals and bed. I had no idea what the purpose of prayer was or why we did it. It was just as easy as breathing for my mom. Prayer was her go-to. If we got hurt or sick, she would pray or call her dad to pray.

When I got to college, I remember calling mom to pray for the big stuff. But I also remember coming to a place in my life that she wasn't there to do it, so I would pray in my head. I realized that prayer was something that brought me peace. I had no idea why, but it did. Now that I am older, I can see how it all makes sense.

When Matt and I started dating and got married, he was the one who would pray for us. We would pray before a meal or when we had an issue or decision to make. In the mornings before he left for work, we would stand together and hold hands, and he would cover our day in prayer. I'd never seen that before. My parents did not do that, but my husband's parents did.

Not until we were married a while and started helping other people did I really start praying. Once I started, it was like a dam broke loose. I realized the power we have by just saying a few words.

Prayer connects us to God.

Talking to God really is as easy as talking to your friend or your spouse. The more you talk to Him, the more you get to know Him. He already knows you because He created you, but the more you pray, the more He gets to know you as well. Prayer is the pathway to the heart of God. You walk a little toward Him, and He comes and meets you there. You share what is on your heart, your concerns, your hurts, your desires, and God listens.

Anytime you talk and share your life with anyone, a connection forms. The same is true with you and God as a result of prayer. Most of the time when people pray, they just speak their minds, ask for a couple of things, and move on. That is fine, whatever it takes to get the conversation going. God is always listening. He is always there waiting when you need to talk.

The more praying you do, the more connected you feel. Think of any relationship you have. The more you talk and get to know each other, the closer you become. Prayer does the same thing. It connects your heart to God's heart. Over time prayer will become something you want to do because you will want to spend time with the Lord.

Prayer brings us peace.

Most nights I pray myself to sleep. Whether it is a prayer over my kids and family or things that are on my heart, I lie in bed at night and just pray. Sometimes I talk the whole time, and sometimes I listen. I like to get the day's stuff off my chest and relax. Prayer is my way of letting it all go so I can sleep peacefully.

Stressful situations are hard on all of us. We usually try to fix them ourselves, and we get overwhelmed. If we can learn to pray in those moments, peace will come. Philippians 4:6–7 says, "Do not be anxious about anything, but in every situation, by prayer and petition, with thanksgiving, present your requests to God. And the peace of God, which transcends all understanding, will guard your hearts and your minds in Christ Jesus" (NIV).

Whether it is work, home, school, sickness or emotional pain, pray. If we are afraid, we can pray. God's Word tells us to call on Him in prayer, and He will give us the peace we need to handle the situation. Peace to manage a hard day. Peace to sleep through the night. Peace to have the hard conversations. Talking to God in prayer brings us peace.

Prayer causes us to rely on God.

When I was pregnant with our boys, I would pray all the time. I would pray over every single ligament, bone, system—every single part that I could possibly think about. I didn't really know what to do; I just talked to Jesus. I asked Him for healthy babies, a healthy body and delivery for me, and all the things. I did this with all three of my pregnancies.

During that time, I talked more than I listened. But God listened.

He taught me He was always there, ready to listen. He drew me in and wooed me to His heart. I became more interested in spending time with Him. I decided to trust Him with the things that worried me. I began to really give Him my heart.

When the boys were babies and toddlers, I would pray for them when they were sick. I didn't know how to pray; I just started talking to Jesus. Sometimes I begged Him to heal them because they were sick with a fever and we were both exhausted.

Later, I began to anoint them with oil in the shape of a cross on their foreheads and pray God's Word over them. I began to remind God of what His Word said, and in turn I reminded myself. Each time, I grew a little more confident that He was listening and that He was their healer.

> SITTING IN HIS PRESENCE AND LETTING HIM TEACH YOU TO PRAY AND TRUST HIM—HERE IS WHERE YOU FIND OUT WHAT FULL RELIANCE IS. HERE IS WHERE YOU FIND TRUE HOPE.

During those sickness struggles, I learned to trust a little more each time. In those moments, I was desperate for a touch from Him. Little did I know, I was preparing my heart to trust Him in even harder times. He was teaching me to rely on Him even if we did not receive the healing or answer we needed.

There is a powerful song called "Living Hope" by Phil Wickham that speaks of Jesus Christ being our living hope in desperate times. Pull it up on your favorite music streaming app.

I believe that learning to rely on God through prayer is your path to finding hope. Learning to speak from your heart to the Creator of the world, who gave His only Son for you, is surreal. Sit in His presence and let Him teach you to pray and trust Him. Here is where you find out what full reliance is. Here is where you find true hope. A trust is developed here that no man can ever offer you. It is here you find a love like no other. Lean in, rely on Him, sit in His presence, and find all you need. Prayer will do that for you.

Prayer is our lifeline to God. He is always there to listen to us, but He also wants us to learn how to listen.

Prayer relieves the pressure.

Sometimes it feels you are running a marathon when really you are running for your life. The demands of life take their toll over time. Work, finances and bills, expectations, child-rearing, sick kids, rude teenagers, parents and in-laws, family dinners, adult children with spouses—and these aren't even the pressures from outside such as technology and the changing culture.

The workforce is dog-eat-dog, and so is the car line at school. It's a constant that doesn't stop; it just changes as your seasons change. In every season, we have to make time to stop. The world will not stop for you. You have to plan your time to stop, because the run for your life will catch up with you if you don't slow down for a breather.

This is when the Bible says to be still. Psalm 46:10 says, "Be still, and know that I am God."

We have to find the calm. There is only One who has the authority to command the wind and the waves and tell the sun and moon when to rise and set. He is the calm. The world does not offer anything that brings the calm. The world will tell you to be you, live your truth, find your calm. God is the only One who can give you true peace and calm. He is the peacekeeper. He holds peace because it is His nature. "You will keep him [or her] in perfect peace, whose mind is stayed on You, because he [or she] trusts in You" (Isa. 26:3).

He commands the waves and the storm to cease in Mark 4:39 by using the words, "Peace, be still!" He is the only One who can relieve the pressure. He is the calm when the storms of life try to take you down. Prayer is the place to find that peace and calm.

I had a Bible study leader once named Bethany Funderburk, who was a bit older than me. She led a group called Titus 2 at our church. She shared a prayer with us that I have prayed a million times when I've been about to lose it. I wish I knew how to credit her for this and say thank you.

As mentioned before, in Psalm 46:10 God reminds us, "Be still, and know that I am God." We are going to take these words and use them to calm our hearts, minds, and spirits.

Find a place to stop, lie down, sit down, turn off all the noise, silence your phone, or leave it in the other room for ten minutes. If this worries you to leave it for ten minutes, you need this prayer. God will cover you and yours during your time with Him. Learn to make it a habit. You and Him alone is golden.

1. Say the words slowly, "Be still, and know that I am God."

   Think about what that sentence means to you, and begin to think about God and all He has done and who He is to you and for you. Once you process that, your stress will start to dwindle.

2. Take the last word off and say this slowly, "Be still, and know that I am."

   Think about that. He is the great I Am, the Creator of the universe, the One who formed you in your mother's womb and knew you before you were a glimpse in your parents' thoughts. He is I Am, and you are His. Ponder the "I Am" for a minute.

3. Next we are going to remove "am." Say slowly, "Be still, and know that I..."

   Think about the rest of this sentence. Find awe in God and all He is to you. Allow peace to seep in.

4. Let's remove "I." Say slowly, "Be still, and know that..."

   Let God fill in the blanks of all He is doing in you. Lean in, listen, and be filled with His love.

5. "That" is gone. Slowly speak, "Be still, and know..."

   Focus on what the great I Am wants you to know. Stop talking, and listen; let Him fill you.

6. Delete "know." Say slowly, "Be still, and..."
   Meet Him there, my friend. Press in.

7. The "and" is no more. Just "be still."
   Find peace from your Father, and just be still.

8. Now, just "be."
   Sit here as long as you need.

The person who began this prayer is no more. Your spirit and mind are set on Him now, my friend. Get up when you feel full, and return to your day. But don't go until your Daddy releases you. He has done a work. Just be.

15

PRAYER WARRIORS OF THE BIBLE

*T*HE BIBLE IS crowded with people praying. The Old and New Testaments are full of some heavy hitters who went to God with their issues. Some went in desperation; some prayed because they were alone. Some prayed because they needed someone to listen. For whatever reason you may need or want, God is ready to listen.

One of the coolest things about these people in the Bible is where they prayed. This was pretty interesting to research. After you read this, you will know the proof that God doesn't care about the *where*.

P.S. Grab your Bible and read more about these amazing men and women.

ABRAHAM—THE BOOK OF GENESIS

Abraham has an incredible story, as he is known for his faith. Known as Abram then, he and his wife, Sarai, couldn't have children, and they waited and waited on God to show up. God promised Abram he would be the father of nations. Genesis 15:5 says, "[God] took him outside and said, 'Look up at the sky and count the stars—if indeed you can count them.' Then he said to him, 'So shall your offspring be'" (NIV).

At this point Abram had no children, and he and Sarai were both growing old. In the very next verse Abram did something that made his name known throughout history. Genesis

15:6 says, "Abram believed the LORD, and He credited it to him as righteousness" (MEV).

Abram believed in God—true faith.

Hebrews 11:1 says, "Faith is the substance of things hoped for, the evidence of things not seen."

Abram took God at His word. He didn't doubt what God said was true, and it was a credit to his life. Over the course of many, many years, Abram and Sarai kept waiting. Some crazy stuff happened when they tried to take matters into their own hands. Then, the first recorded prayer in the Bible came from Abraham.

In Genesis 18 the Lord Himself went to visit Abraham and Sarah and tell them to remain in the faith and He would give them a son. By then, they were way too old to even have kids—but God. God was walking with Abraham and a couple of angels, just chatting it up because that was the relationship they had. On that visit from God, they had a discussion about the sin happening in Sodom and Gomorrah.

God pondered whether he should tell Abraham what He was about to do to the sinful city. God knew Abraham would keep the way of the Lord, so God proceeded to tell Abraham His plans.

Now just a side note: Who else wants to be in a relationship with God where He comes over for a visit and tells you His plans? My hand is up! I do! This is what I call a close-knit, trusted bond. Way cool!

After hearing the Lord's plans, Abraham "approached him" and asked God not to kill the righteous in the land (Gen. 18:23, NIV). Abraham pleaded with God. This is the first recorded prayer in the Bible.

It isn't called a prayer, but the situation is different here because God and Abraham were hanging out. Abraham had a "He walks with me" (even literally) relationship with God. He approached

God and pleaded his case, and they met in the middle. Read this story when you can, because it is pretty interesting.

The next time we see Abraham pray, it is out of desperation, mixed with a complete calm no one else in his situation could ever have. Again, it is not called a prayer, because it was different with Abraham.

Abraham believed God in a way most will never know. He heard God's plan and believed—period—so much so that it is considered what makes him righteous. They walked the earth together. God made promises, and Abraham believed. God said it; Abraham waited until it happened.

Abraham's second prayer of sorts comes in the form of a test. His son Isaac was in his teens by then, and God told Abraham to take Isaac to Moriah and sacrifice him there. After waiting one hundred years for his promised son, now God wanted him back. We find this story in Genesis 22.

God told Abraham to take Isaac and sacrifice him. They got up early the next morning, cut the wood for the offering, and took off on their way. They got there, and Abraham and Isaac headed up the mountain. Isaac asked his dad, "The fire and wood are here...but where is the lamb for the burnt offering?" (Gen. 22:7, NIV). Having done this many times in his life, I'm sure Isaac was wondering what was happening. I know I would be.

Genesis 22:8 mentions Abraham's answer, "God himself will provide the lamb for the burnt offering, my son." Isaac believed his dad and kept walking. Abraham believed God, again. Believing in something he didn't see, he just knew in his "knower" that God had his back.

If you read on, you see Abraham and Isaac got all the wood ready, then Abraham bound his son with the rope and laid him on top of the wood. OK, back the truck up. I have three boys; I would have to chase them down to be able to tie them up and lay them down on the altar. Holy moly. This is some serious, down-to-the-wire, believing-for-a-miracle faith right here.

As a parent I cannot wrap my head around all the thoughts swirling in Abraham's head. But what about Isaac? That poor kid. He must've thought, "What the heck is happening?" Or maybe as the son of Abraham, he had the same steadfast faith of his father. Either way, he lay there, ready for what was to come.

Verse 10 tells us Abraham even took his knife to slay his son. Wow! This is full-on faith! I would love to know what was going through his mind at that moment. He was one hundred years old when his son was born; now he had to sacrifice him. I have to believe Abraham walked so closely with God his thoughts were connected with the heart of God. I believe he was thinking, "I will trust You no matter what."

As Abraham raised his quivering hand, prepared to slay his son,

> the angel of the LORD called out to him from heaven, "Abraham! Abraham!"
>
> "Here I am," he replied.
>
> "Do not lay a hand on the boy. Do not do anything to him. Now I know that you fear God, because you have not withheld from me your son, your only son."
>
> —GENESIS 22:11–12, NIV

Then, there in the thicket was a ram—provision from heaven for the burnt sacrifice. Unbelievable. Abraham didn't even have to pray in these moments; he just knew God would show up somehow, some way, and boy did He!

The angel of the Lord spoke to Abraham again later and reassured the promise of his descendants being as numerous as the stars in the sky. Why? Because he didn't hold back his son. Abraham did not put his love for his son in front of his love for God. Wow! He is the epitome of Habakkuk 2:4: "the righteous one will live by his faith" (NASB). This is the kind of faith I want to have—to be fully known, fully faithful, fully trusting, and lacking nothing.

MOSES—THE BOOK OF EXODUS

Moses prayed in many weird places. He prayed on a mountain when he saw the burning bush and met the Lord for the first time. Looking in the text of Exodus 3, we see Moses had already left Pharaoh's home in Egypt and was tending the flock of his father-in-law on the mountain of Horeb. Here he met God for the first time. The text does not say, "Moses prayed," but it is clear that Moses was talking to God, which is prayer. Moses hid his face because he was afraid to look at God.

God came and found Moses in the middle of this mountain and called him to be His disciple. Moses wasn't prepared for this. He hid from God. Moses was raised in Pharaoh's home. He wasn't raised to know or believe in God. He was on his merry way, watching his flock, when a bush started burning, but not burning. I'm sure he was like, "What in the world?" Can you imagine seeing a burning bush that wasn't burning or being consumed, and then it starts talking to you? Y'all, I would faint.

This is the first time God spoke to Moses. Moses did not know God at this moment. He got a crash course in salvation and hearing the voice of God. Here, God called Moses to be a leader and do some hard things. Moses wasn't ready. He knew he didn't have what it took to do this. So Moses questioned God. I'm sure none of us have ever done that, right?

But Moses went home, told his wife, and began his faithful path God had for him. He took a huge leap of faith, left his home, and set out on a trip that would show him more miracles than have been recorded before.

Moses doubted himself again later. He wondered if he really

was the right one for the job. Even after seeing God do miracles with his staff, Moses said to the Lord in Exodus 4:13, "Pardon your servant, Lord. Please send someone else." But God provided Moses with a helper in his newfound brother, Aaron. Then the work of God began, with Moses, the unsuspecting shepherd who spoke with God on a mountain.

Moses' prayers didn't stop here. He went through with his calling to lead the Israelites out of Egypt. The people had seen God move. But when they got to the water's edge, they began to be afraid and doubtful. Even regret of leaving Egypt crossed their minds. Moses had to pray to God again at this moment. Do you know where? Moses prayed at the water's edge of the Red Sea. They had nowhere to go. The people were panicking.

Moses prayed to God, and God told Moses to raise his staff to part the sea so the Israelites could cross through. At this moment, I think I would have had similar thoughts to the Israelites: "What have we done? We left our home and are being chased. Now we have to cross this mighty flowing river. We will die." But God. He came through again, with a pillar of cloud by day and a pillar of fire by night—full-blown protection. After they made it through the sea, Moses and Miriam began to praise the Lord for saving them. This is so cool! Have you ever prayed, seen God answer you, and then praised Him for His goodness and provision? Maybe we should. They trusted God before the storm and in the middle of the storm, and praised Him after the storm. What faith!

Now, Moses wasn't done with his weird places to pray. Her are a few more:

- Moses prayed many times in the desert as he and the Israelites wandered around.

- Moses prayed on a mountain when he met God to get the Ten Commandments and met with God on Mount Sinai.

- Moses prayed to God in the wilderness for food and provision.

- Moses prayed again in the wilderness as he was building the tabernacle, for the ark of the covenant. Moses spoke with God and built the ark of the covenant specifically as God had said.

Moses started as a man who did not know God, but God called him to do something amazing. He became a man who sought after God. He became a man who prayed to God all the time and desired the things of God daily. Moses is a good example of a person who can pray anywhere. God met him where he was and established a covenant with Moses that has impacted our history and our future.

Moses prayed from a place of insecurity, fear, and frustration. God met him where he was and gave him what he needed. God can take an ordinary man and make him extraordinary. Do Moses' prayers seem to come from a familiar place to you? God is where you are.

HOSEA—THE BOOK OF HOSEA

Hosea is one of those people who deserved his own book in the most famous historical book of all time. In studying Hosea, I found his name means "salvation." Hosea was a prophet. He was a man of God. Hosea was called by God to marry an adulterous wife. She bore him children, then ran off again in adultery.

Hosea prayed to God at home and as he searched for her in the city. He found her and paid for her and took her home, even after she was unfaithful to him. Hosea's life and his forgiveness for his wife's unfaithfulness were symbolic of God's love for the Israelites even when they were unfaithful to God. Have you ever prayed when you were unfaithful, or have you been treated unfaithfully? Have you ever prayed for forgiveness or been given forgiveness?

Hosea prayed from a place of betrayal, anger, and frustration. He prayed for the ability to forgive and for repentance to be in his heart and his wife's. God is faithful to the unfaithful. God forgives a repentant heart. God is ready to forgive, ready to prove Himself faithful. Do you need to pray from this place?

JONAH—THE BOOK OF JONAH

Even if you don't know much about the Bible, many have heard about Jonah and the phenomenon that is his story. Jonah prayed from inside the belly of a big fish. If this isn't the weirdest place so far, I don't know where is.

His story starts with God telling him to go and do something, and he runs the other way. Jonah blatantly disobeyed God. Really, Jonah? He went the other direction, thinking he could hide from God. He ran from God. He ran from his calling. Can you really hide from God? Jonah tried.

Jonah took a ship headed in another direction from what God had told him to do. God was like, "Um, no; I told you to go to Nineveh, not Tarshish." So God sent a storm. The sailors were afraid and started throwing cargo overboard while Jonah slept below deck. The sailors went down and asked him to pray. They wanted to know who was at fault. They found out it was him, and Jonah said, "Throw me over; this is all my fault."

Then the sailors prayed to Jonah's God. On a boat, in the midst of a major storm, they prayed to a God they didn't know, for Him to not hold them accountable for this man's life. The sailors then took Jonah and threw him overboard. God brought a giant fish to swallow Jonah up.

For three days and three nights, Jonah was inside the fish when he prayed. He asked God to hear his cry of distress. Then he thanked God for bringing his life up from the pit (Jon. 2:6). Whew! Can you imagine this? I have been in many storms in life. I have been at fault for things happening to me and others. I have disobeyed God's direct orders. I haven't ever been swallowed up by a fish, but sometimes it feels as if life swallows you up.

Have you ever been in this place of prayer? Have you ever prayed to God in distress? Have you ever needed God to pull your life up from the pit? Jonah's place of disobedience, distress, and drowning may be real to you. God hears your cries from this place. He's waiting for you to come. Stop running. His plan is always best. Believe me.

JOSHUA—THE BOOK OF NUMBERS

Joshua is the guy who took over after Moses died. Joshua was actually around a while before we realized who he was. Moses changed his name in Numbers 13:16 from Hoshea to Joshua. It floored me when I discovered this. Hoshea means "He is salvation"; Joshua means "God is salvation." Just as God changed Abram's name to Abraham and his wife, Sarai, to Sarah, Joshua got a new name because of his faith in God. He is called Joshua when we first meet him in most versions of the Bible, but my notes from Exodus 17:9 explain that Joshua was formerly Hoshea son of Nun.

I want to look first at a time when Joshua needed his own prayers and the prayers of another. We find Joshua praying on the battlefield as he fights. In chapter 17 of the Book of Exodus, Joshua was the man chosen to fight the Amalekite army. Moses told Joshua to choose some men and go and fight. Moses told him he would stand at the top of the hill with the staff of God in his hands. The next morning, Joshua and his army went out to fight, and they fought hard. Moses took his place of prayer on the top of the hill, watching over where the war was going on. When Moses' hands were raised and his staff was up, Joshua was winning. When Moses' arms fell, the Amalekites would start winning.

The war went on all day, and Moses began to get tired. This is the moment when Aaron and Hur had to help by holding up Moses' arms. Moses sat on a stone to rest, and Aaron and Hur held up his arms. All. Day. Long. They held up his arms until sunset, when Joshua overcame the Amalekite army. The Lord told Moses in verse 14, "Write this on a scroll as something to be remembered and make sure that Joshua hears it" (NIV). So Moses wrote it on a scroll and made an altar to remember the moment of God's power and favor. He called it The Lord Is My Banner because hands were lifted up to the throne of God. This reminds me of worship. You lift your hands, asking Daddy God to help you, hold you, take care of it, and He shows up.

Moses is raising his staff, with the help of Aaron and Hur, and God of course. Joshua is in the battle, praying as he fights. Joshua is depending on the prayers of Moses up above him on a hill, sitting on a rock, holding the staff of God all day. Have you ever prayed all day for another person? Moses, Aaron, and Hur were praying for Joshua and the army all day. They were trusting God to intervene and watched as He did. If you haven't prayed all day for your spouse, your kids, or anyone, you should consider it. It is life-giving sacrificing your time for another person. This story is a selfless act of prayer *by* Moses *for* Joshua and his army. So cool! What person does God want you to sacrifice in prayer for?

We are not finished with Joshua. He prays in another place that seems odd, but most of us know this story. We find ourselves in the Book of Joshua. The Israelites had still not made it to the Promised Land, but Joshua planned to. God made some awesome promises to Joshua. Look at Joshua 1:5: "No one will be able to stand against you all the days of your life. As I was with Moses, so I will be with you; I will never leave you nor forsake you. Be strong and courageous, because you will lead these people to inherit the land" (NIV). Joshua was chosen because God knew he would obey the Lord and the Book of the Law.

Joshua was a wise man. Having taken over as Moses' successor, he had big shoes to fill. Not only shoes, but the promise from God was about to be fulfilled. Joshua gave the Israelites a few days' notice that they would be traveling so they could get ready.

The Israelites told Joshua in verses 16–17, "All that you have commanded us we will do, and wherever you send us we will go. Just as we obeyed Moses in all things, so we will obey you" (NASB). The Israelites trusted Joshua as they had Moses; they knew he heard from God and wouldn't lead them astray.

Joshua secretly sent spies ahead to make sure they were good to enter Jericho. Inside the walls of Jericho there was a prostitute named Rahab. She took care of and hid the spies because she had heard about their God. In return for her hiding the spies, she asked for them to return the favor and remember her and her family when they penetrated the city. Hearing from Rahab that the people of Jericho were afraid, the spies knew God would help them prevail.

The spies returned to the Israelite camp and stayed several days. Joshua waited on God to tell him when. He was patiently listening. When God said, Joshua knew it was time to move. I'm sure many prayers were lifted up at that campsite regarding the coming days. The Israelites were instructed to follow the ark of the covenant wherever it went because that was the place of God's presence. Their instructions were to follow the presence of God, because where the presence of the Lord is, mighty things happen.

Finding them in Joshua 3, Joshua asks the people to conse-crate (purify) themselves before the journey so the Lord would do amazing things among them. Joshua believed God would do what He said He would do. This was a time for them to pray, ask for forgiveness, and possibly make a sacrifice.

Consecration is purifying yourself from anything that could separate you from your relationship with God. They probably bathed and changed clothes as a symbol of starting fresh. Joshua needed everyone prepared and sanctified so that God would show off. The Israelites' ancestors had witnessed God showing off and doing amazing miracles, but some of this generation had only heard the tales.

The forty years of roaming was coming to an end. The prayers of their forefathers had not gone unanswered but had been delayed for such a time as this. This generation was waiting to see God show off and do something amazing. The time to follow God was now.

The next morning, the men carrying the ark got to the water's edge. Miraculously, the Jordan River, being at flood stage, stopped flowing upstream. The people crossed over it into Jericho with no problems. After they crossed the Jordan River, God told Joshua to have twelve men place twelve stones in the water at the place they had crossed and consecrate that spot as a memorial to God for future generations to know what God had done there. God did something amazing, as Joshua expected.

They had probably heard the stories of when the Lord parted the Red Sea for their ancestors fleeing the Egyptians, but never expected to see it with their own eyes. Once they were all out of the water, the waters began to flow once more. Joshua had prayed at camp for a huge miracle to take place, and it did. Joshua and the Israelites probably prayed as they crossed as well—I know I would.

God then told Joshua to do something that looked and sounded crazy. Joshua prayed and got specific directions. He followed perfectly the direction of the angel of the Lord. They all marched around the walls of the city of Jericho quietly for six days. On the seventh day the priest sounded the trumpet and Joshua commanded the people, "Shout! For the LORD has given you the city!" (Josh. 6:16, NIV). The walls collapsed, and the Israelites took the city and consecrated it to the Lord.

Joshua prayed as he led the armies in battle to take Jericho and many cities after that. He was a man of faith toward God. He knew God would do what He promised. Joshua didn't like some of the actions of his people, because he loved God more than anything else.

Joshua prayed from a place of leadership and a place of trust in God. He followed the presence of the Lord into what could have been a dangerous situation. Regardless of what would come, he trusted God's faithfulness.

Do you follow the Lord wholeheartedly? Do you walk in a manner that leads others to follow God? Do you pray from a place of trusting God fully? Have you seen God do miracles?

Joshua prayed from a place of trust, leadership, and believing God would do what He said He would do. Have you come to that place? Do you believe God can work miracles in your life? Joshua did.

ESTHER—THE BOOK OF ESTHER

Esther was chosen to do something amazing. God's timing had to be spot-on for her story to unfold, and as always He came through. Let's take a look at this together, finding Esther in the book after her own name. God's plan began to unfold when the present queen decided she didn't want to be queen and refused the king. In an effort to keep all wives from being disrespectful, she was removed from her post, and the search for a new queen was upon them.

A Jewish man named Mordecai had raised his beautiful female cousin Hadassah, who was also known as Esther. When the call came out for the virgins of the land to come to the palace and be presented before the king, God's perfect plan continued. Mordecai had to convince Esther, but she went out of obedience and respect.

Esther was given beauty treatments, along with the other girls, and when she was presented to the king, the Bible says in Esther 2:9, "She pleased him and won his favor" (NIV). Esther was surprised she had won the king's favor, for she was of Jewish descent. Mordecai had forbidden her to reveal her nationality, but she followed the plans of the kingdom and found favor with the king.

A plan was created to kill all the Jews; Mordecai passed the information along to Esther. Mordecai told Esther, "Perhaps you have come to your royal position for such a time as this" (Est. 4:14, CSB). Esther knew she had to speak with the king and prevent the annihilation of the Jews. So Esther asked Mordecai and the Jewish people to fast for her. This was her requesting her people to pray for favor for her as she met with the king. Esther set up the meeting with the king and a man named Haman, who planned to kill the Jews.

Knowing she was going to meet with the king and expose the bad guy, Esther needed to be covered in prayer. Her family was covering her while hiding from the man who wanted them all murdered. Surely, she prayed for favor and courage in the midst of all the beauty treatments in the palace. She presented her request to the king and exposed Haman's plan. She also found favor with the king, and her family was protected. She reminded the king of a good man's kindness, and her uncle Mordecai was regarded for helping the kingdom.

Esther found favor, all the while being covered in prayer by her family. Esther needed the help from her family, and they needed her help to keep them safe. When both sides step in to support one another, big things can happen. Life's occurrences bring us to moments when we need to call in reinforcements. We need others to pray with us, no matter where it is. Have you ever found yourself in a place where you needed someone else to hold you up in prayer? Do you have people you can call? Asking people for help and support is not weakness; it is part of what makes the body of Christ work as it was created.

DANIEL—THE BOOK OF DANIEL

Daniel prayed in a lions' den. Most people know the story of Daniel in the lions' den. But that's not the beginning of this story. Daniel worked his way up to a place of trust and faith in God. Daniel's story of prayer really starts in Daniel 2.

Daniel lived in Babylon during the reign of King Nebuchadnezzar. He had made himself known in the town and in the kingdom. When King Nebuchadnezzar wanted a dream to be interpreted, he asked the magicians and astrologers to do it, and they couldn't. In fact, they said there was not a man on this earth who could do what the king asked (Dan. 2:10).

The king got so mad at them for not being able to interpret the dream that he had them all executed. Daniel thought that was pretty harsh, so he asked the king for some time so he might interpret the dream for him.

Daniel ran home, gathered his friends, and said, "Let's pray." See Daniel 2:16–23. The Bible says Daniel prayed and "urged them to plead for mercy from the God of heaven concerning this mystery" (NIV). You see, in Daniel 1, Daniel and his buddies had already proved themselves and God had given them knowledge and understanding as a gift. God had also given

Daniel the ability to understand visions and dreams of all kinds (Dan. 1:17).

Daniel knew God heard his prayers. Daniel had God's confidence. He had confidence in God to answer Him because he had a relationship with Him. So Daniel prayed, believing God would hear and answer. He went to bed with peaceful trust and awoke with a revelation from God.

Daniel 2:19 says, "During the night the mystery was revealed to Daniel in a vision." Then Daniel praised God in the next couple of verses for all that God is. After the revelation Daniel was able to go back in to meet with the king and interpret his dream. His revelation came from God, and as a result, Daniel saved his own life and the lives of his friends.

What's really cool is that over time King Nebuchadnezzar continued to trust Daniel to interpret the dreams for him and realized God was the One doing it. Daniel's faith spoke to the king and changed his heart.

Now let's go a little deeper and see how Daniel got to the point of trust in his prayers to God. The famous story of Daniel in the lions' den falls after the story of the dream interpretation, but it gives us insight into the lifestyle of Daniel.

Daniel lived a lifestyle of prayer.

Let's see what that looks like by taking a look in Daniel 6. King Darius was on the throne in Babylon. Daniel was very well loved by the king because of his qualities (Dan. 6:3). The other leaders in town hated him for it and didn't want him to be in charge, so they plotted against him.

They knew there was nothing to charge him with unless it had to do with his faith in God (vv. 4–5).

These men went to the king and used his pride against him. They wanted him to issue a decree saying that all men should pray only to the king and no one else. The king loved this idea, so he issued and signed a decree (vv. 6–9).

Daniel's lifestyle of prayer is revealed at this moment (vv. 10–11). Daniel heard about the decree, and he went home and prayed to God as he normally did, falling on his knees, three times a day.

Daniel prayed with the windows open. He didn't worry about being seen. He wasn't trying to hide. He wasn't trying to say, "I'll show you and do what I want." Daniel was just doing his thing. He didn't let a decree or fear take away what he had with the Father God.

The story goes on to tell us that the king had to throw him into the lions' den even though he didn't want to because Daniel disobeyed the king's decree (vv. 13–16).

In vv. 16–28, King Darius tried everything he could to keep from having to put Daniel in the lions' den. But he had to follow his own rule.

Daniel was thrown into the lions' den, and they even put a large stone on top to seal it, believing he was sealing Daniel's fate. The king was stressed out and could not sleep all night.

In verse 20 we find the king running to the den the next morning, calling out for Daniel in anguish, "Daniel, servant of the living God, has your God, whom you serve continually, been able to rescue you from the lions?" (NIV).

In verse 22 Daniel answered, "My God sent his angel, and he shut the mouths of the lions. They have not hurt me, because I was found innocent in his sight" (NIV). King Darius was so happy to hear Daniel's response, proving he was alive. The king pulled Daniel out, and verse 23 says, "No wound was found on him, because he had trusted in his God." Wow! This is so amazing—Daniel trusted God and was protected by God's angels. This is the coolest thing!

Not only did Daniel's accusers get thrown in the lions' den, but King Darius changed the decree to make sure people prayed to God. In verses 26–27, King Darius said, "I issue a decree that in every part of my kingdom people must fear and reverence the God of Daniel. For he is the living God and he endures forever; his kingdom will not be destroyed, his dominion will never end. He rescues and he saves; he performs signs and wonders in the heavens and on the earth. He has rescued Daniel from the power of the lions" (NIV).

One man's faith can change an entire nation, or town, or school. Daniel's relationship with God through prayer gave him the confidence he needed to pray when he wasn't supposed to. He trusted God would save him when there seemed to be no way out. Daniel didn't just happen upon this deep trust and faith in God. It came at a price. Daniel spent time with the Lord regularly, and it paid off.

Are you willing to give up your time and spend some of it with God in prayer and/or reading His Word? Do you think doing so would grow your faith and trust in God and what He can do? Wouldn't you like to live with God's confidence like Daniel? Do you have faith you can share and make a difference where you live or work?

HANNAH—THE BOOK OF 1 SAMUEL

Hannah is one of those women of the Bible you may or may not have heard of. Her story is wedged in the middle of the Old Testament in 1 Samuel 1. She was married to a man who truly loved her named Elkanah. He was a devout man of faith who went to Shiloh to worship and make a sacrifice to the Lord Almighty.

Elkanah had two wives, Peninnah and Hannah. Peninnah had given him several children, but Hannah's womb was barren. After his sacrifice, Elkanah gave Hannah a double portion because he loved her. What a good man.

Hannah endured years and years of torment and pro-voking from Peninnah. She was so unkind she led Hannah to tears again and again. Elkanah would find her and love on her and remind her how much she was loved regardless of her barrenness.

On a trip to the temple in Shiloh, Hannah once again was provoked unto tears and fled the room. First Samuel 1:10–11 says, "She was in bitterness of soul, and prayed to the LORD and wept in anguish. Then she made a vow." Hannah prayed and asked the almighty Lord to look upon her misery and give her a son, and she promised to give him to the Lord for all the days of his life. The Lord heard her prayers and gave her a son. She named the boy Samuel, which means "God heard," because she asked the Lord for him and He heard her.

Hannah fulfilled her promise to the Lord, who fulfilled His promise to her. Once the boy was weaned, she took him to the temple to dedicate him to the Lord. She took the boy to Eli the high priest and reminded him of who she was. Verses 27–28 say, "I prayed for this child, and the LORD has granted me what I asked of him. So now I give him to the LORD. For his whole life he will be given over to the LORD."

My momma heart wants to burst into tears for this woman. She was so downcast her whole married life until God gave her all she asked. Then, she had to give him back. This is sim-ilar to what we do as Christian parents; we dedicate our chil-dren to the Lord when they are young. We pray over them and ask God to take care of them and help us raise them to know and serve Him with their lives. It's similar but not the same. She had to leave her young son and go home without him. Ugh, this is gut-wrenching.

Here's the best part about Hannah: her faith and trust. First Samuel 2:1–10 is called Hannah's Prayer. This woman is a rock star. She made a vow, and she kept it. She promised to take him to the church and let him serve God fully. But before she left Samuel, she covered him in prayer and thanked God for His gracious gift. Grab your Bible and take a moment to read Hannah's Prayer in 1 Samuel 2. It is known as a song of praise and a prophecy about what God would do through her son Samuel. Wow! This woman is strong and mighty.

The first time, Hannah prayed from a place of bitterness, sadness, emptiness, and desperation. She begged God and made a promise to Him, and He fulfilled it. Then, she had to do the same.

The second time she prayed, she prayed from a place of praise, fulfillment, and trust in God's plans and promises. She praised God for fulfilling His promise and hoped with full faith that God would do exceedingly more than she asked of Him through her son Samuel.

She left Samuel in the hands of Eli and in the hands of God. She came to visit each time Elkanah came to the temple to worship. Each time, Eli prayed for them and God opened Hannah's womb and gave her and Elkanah more children. Samuel remained at the temple, and he "grew up in the presence of the LORD" (1 Sam. 2:21).

Prayer completely changed Hannah for the better. When she fell at the feet of the Lord in desperation, He met her there and the healing began. He answered her prayers, and she became devoted to Him from that moment on.

Do you think to go to the Father from a place of desperation? Do you believe He will hear you? Do you think if He answered your prayer, you would devote your life to Him? What about if He didn't answer your prayers? Are you still willing to trust Him? Are you willing to spend time with God in prayer and see if He meets you there?

HEZEKIAH—THE BOOK OF 2 KINGS

Hezekiah is one of the kings in the Old Testament. He is wedged nicely near the end of 2 Kings. You have to get to him by reading about all the kings. He is first seen in 2 Kings 18. He became king at twenty-five years old and followed the Lord. The Bible describes each king with either "He did what was right in the eyes of the Lord," or, "He did evil in the sight of the Lord." Hezekiah was one of the sons of David, and he followed the Lord as his father did. All of David's sons were not servants of the Lord.

Hezekiah's reign started off with the Assyrian King Sennacherib announcing to everyone not to listen to Hezekiah. He mocked Hezekiah and ran his name in the mud and acted as if their trust in the Lord was foolish. The guy kept at it, and Hezekiah went up to the house of the Lord to pray. He basically just glorified God in this prayer and asked God to save them. Whatever he said worked, and God moved.

Second Kings 19:35 says, "On that night the angel of the LORD went out and struck one hundred and eighty-five thousand in the camp of the Assyrians" (MEV). Everyone else woke to find their dead friends. Then, King Sennacherib went to worship his gods, and his own sons came in and killed him.

What?

Y'all, Hezekiah prayed, and he didn't even have to send his army. God handled it for him. Then, the mean king was killed by his own sons. That is some serious praying.

It doesn't end there. Later on, King Hezekiah got sick and was about to die. We find him in this state in 2 Kings 20. The Lord told the prophet Isaiah to go and tell King Hezekiah to get his affairs in order. Hezekiah heard the news and turned his face to the wall and prayed a reminder prayer to God of how faithful he had been to God. He had done what was good in God's sight and had an undivided heart. He wept and pleaded with God and reminded God of the promises he had given to Hezekiah.

Before Isaiah could even leave the courtyard of the palace, God spoke to him to turn around and go back to Hezekiah. Here is what God had Isaiah say: "Thus says the LORD, the God of David your father: I have heard your prayer; I have seen your tears. I will heal you" (MEV). God gave Hezekiah victory over Assyria, and He gave him another fifteen years to live. But that's not all.

The sign for King Hezekiah's healing would come on the third day. Isaiah gave Hezekiah a paste to make out of figs and use on his boils to heal himself. After that, on the third day, God moved the sun's shadow back ten steps as a sign to show Hezekiah He would do as He said.

If you ever doubt God hears your prayers and will move on your behalf, use the faith of Hezekiah to remind yourself God does more than we can even dream when we pray. His prayers were just a cry to the God whom he knew and trusted. They were for different reasons and had different tones and requests. God heard them both.

OTHER OUTSTANDING PRAYER WARRIORS

Here are a few more brief examples of Bible characters who made prayer a priority:

Ruth prayed from a place of loss and loneliness, and God provided food, a job, and a new husband to love in Boaz, her kinsman redeemer.

Job still prayed after losing everyone he loved and cared for. Although he lost all his earthly treasures, he never lost his faith and trust in God. Then, God restored all he had lost and more.

David prayed in a cave, hiding from a man who was once his friend who now wanted him dead.

Noah prayed on a boat, knowing he and his family were the only people on Earth who were still alive, wondering how it would all turn out.

Deborah prayed to the Lord for wisdom as she was a judge to the town and a prophet of God. This was rare for women in her time. Even the leader of the army didn't want to go to battle without Deborah there because she was such a powerhouse. Sisera fell to the hands of a woman. The village was lifeless until Deborah took her place as judge and prophet and mother to the village, declaring they bless the Lord and not the idols (Judg. 4–5).

Gideon prayed to God about fighting a battle. He was called by the angel of the Lord to save the Israelites and battle the Midianites. To be sure it was the will of the Lord, Gideon set out a fleece three different times to make sure God was speaking, and God answered all three times as Gideon asked. Then, Gideon asked God to help him choose an army. The men numbered twenty-two thousand, and God reduced them down to three hundred men, and Gideon trusted God to defeat a large army with the chosen three hundred men. Even when Gideon doubts God and does a double and triple check to be sure, God is patient with him. Gideon served God in the time of Baal and was successful finding peace for Israel and winning the battle with the Lord's help (Judg. 6–8).

Elijah was a prophet during the reign of an idolatrous King Ahab and his wicked wife, Jezebel. Elijah saw miracle after miracle when he prophesied a drought for three years and prayed for God to stop the rain. He was starving and prayed God would supply enough oil for a widow and her son to have their barrels never dry up. Then the widow's son died and Elijah lay on him three times and called on God to bring him back to life. Later, Elijah called God to bring the rain back after the drought, and when he saw only a small cloud, he knew God had answered his prayer. Elijah prayed and believed God would consume all the water at the sacrifice when he was competing with 450 Baal prophets for God to show up. Our God did show up, and the fire of the Lord licked up the entire sacrifice. Elijah is a major boss in the Old Testament, and his faith and trust in God were paramount. His stories are in 1 Kings and 2 Kings.

Paul prayed from the dungeons of a prison for Jesus' name to be made known. He found joy in his tribulation, worshipping a God whom he used to curse. Paul and Silas sang praises to God and prayed while they were shackled in prison. This caused a great earthquake that shook the prison. The doors opened, and the bonds unfastened. This rocked the prison guard so much he got saved in that moment. Paul was once a persecutor of Christians, until Jesus met him and changed his heart and his life. He had a full transformation all because of his relationship with God.

> NO MATTER WHERE YOU ARE COMING FROM OR WHERE YOU GO TO PRAY, GOD IS PRESENT. REGARDLESS OF WHY YOU NEED TO PRAY, GOD WILL LISTEN. HE IS WAITING ON YOU.

Jesus prayed in the desert while He was being tempted by Satan and drawing life only from listening to the Father and knowing He wasn't alone in the trial.

Jesus prayed in a garden while His friends slept; He prayed with such distress His sweat turned to blood.

Jesus taught his friends the importance of going away from the crowd to get alone with God and pray. He also showed them how to pray with the Lord's Prayer.

Most of these characters in the Bible lived a lifestyle of prayer. But they didn't start there. We have seen so many representations of different people with different reasons to go to the Lord in prayer. Everyone listed here has a unique story, just as you and I do. The place they prayed in, or from, led them on the path that became their *why* for prayer.

Have you made it there yet? Do you know the place from which you have decided that prayer is a necessity for you in your life?

No matter where you are coming from or where you go to pray, God is present. Regardless of why you need to pray, God will listen. He is waiting on you.

16

WHAT DOES A QUIET TIME LOOK LIKE?

*When you pray, go into your room and
shut the door and pray to your Father
who is in secret. And your father who
sees in secret will reward you.*
—MATTHEW 6:6, ESV

WE HAVE SEEN how prayer has a life-changing impact on anyone who does it. We can pray for any reason at all. We can pray from any place at all. We just know we need to pray. We have seen Jesus' explanation of how to pray as well as His example of actual prayer.

Now we know how important prayer is in building your relationship with the heavenly Father—not to mention the necessity of prayer to just make it through the trials of this life.

Any time you can spend with the Lord is good. When I say spend time with the Lord, I mean pray to Him, read the Bible, sing praises to Him. Get quiet, forget about the world around you, and pray. Some call this a quiet time because you get quiet and spend time with the Lord in prayer.

The term *quiet time* scares some people because they don't know how to do one. People don't like the term because they have been judged for not having one, or think it sounds too churchy. Don't let the term scare you. Let's talk about having a quiet time, but let's remember it's just a time of prayer.

Pressure floods in when people ask these questions: "Have you had your quiet time today?" or, "When do you have a quiet time?," "Where do you have your quiet time?," or even,

"How long is your quiet time?" These questions cause people to feel judged by others and get down on themselves because they do not feel as spiritual as their friends.

Nope, not true. However, it doesn't change the fact that comments can cause you to take a look at yourself or even make a decision to not have one because of all the judgment.

There are so many angles by which you can look at a quiet time. *Quiet time* is a term used in the church to represent spending time in the presence of the Lord. There are many rules people think they have to follow, but the Lord doesn't give a set of quiet time rules. I've never seen a Top Ten Quiet Time Commandments anywhere. God just wants to spend time with you. If you make it about rules or following how someone else does it, you won't want to do it.

Don't let the term *quiet time* scare you. Don't let how someone else does it or what they say deter you from your time with the Lord. If you think of your time with the Lord as if making a new friend and reading a novel together, it all seems less daunting. Jesus is a pretty cool friend. And the Bible is an interesting murder mystery, with drama, romance, and intrigue. It's all the genres in one, not to mention it's the greatest love story ever written.

The main thing is to rid yourself of distractions so you can focus on hearing God and meeting with Him. Put your phone on silent or do not disturb. Or leave it in the other room. Just find a place and a time you can focus for a little bit. You will not regret setting the time aside.

Quiet time bonuses:

- Spending time with the Lord is a privilege.
  We live in a country that allows us freedom of religion. We are able to join together in our church home to worship and learn together.

We have the Word of God at our fingertips with podcasts and apps on our phones and devices. Use what you have been blessed with.

- Prayer doesn't have to look a certain way.

  We have already seen that prayers can be short or long. There is no specific way you have to pray. There is no specific time or place you have to pray. Prayer is talking to God. God doesn't care; just pray.

- Spending time with the Lord is just like hanging with a friend.

  There is no pressure, no rules, just you and your heavenly Father, working at building a friendship. You talk; He talks through His Word. It's that easy.

- Quiet time is time with God.

  Our lives and schedules are all different. What works for one may not work for another. Do what you can, when you can. Get quiet and alone with the Lord when it works for you.

- Make your time with the Lord yours.

  Your time with the Lord can be unique. You are. You can sing, read the Bible, listen to a pastor, or just pray. Make it yours.

- The time of day is not His concern; the time together is.

  He just wants you, however He can get you.

Your time may be short and sweet to begin with, and that's OK. The more you spend time with Him, the more time you will want to spend. Making this a time that works for you and fits your life makes it a habit you can get used to. If you attempt something impossible and fail, you will get down on yourself and quit. There are no specific criteria. Do what works for you, and enjoy it!

Your time with the Lord can be unique to you. You can do it however you want. Here are some ideas of things I've heard over time.

Are you a singer? Some people prefer worship music and spend their time with the Lord praising Him, listening and singing to Him. Worship can take you into the presence of the Lord quickly. You will feel close to Him just by singing praises to Him.

Are you a Bible reader and like to research? Some people have ten reference books in front of them with their Bible. Researchers spend their time digging into the meaning of things and translating from the Hebrew and Greek. If you are a researcher, study and seek Him out. Dig in, learn, and have fun doing it!

> *THE MORE YOU SPEND TIME WITH HIM, THE MORE TIME YOU WILL WANT TO SPEND. MAKING THIS A TIME THAT WORKS FOR YOU AND FITS YOUR LIFE MAKES IT A HABIT YOU CAN GET USED TO.*

Do you have a long commute to work every day? If so, your quiet time may be in the car. You can turn on some worship music and sing to the Lord. Then pray and talk to Him as though He's in the car with you. Get quiet and see what He has to say back. Use your device as your Bible. You can use a search engine or find an app to use. Pull up a favorite preacher and listen to a sermon or podcast as you drive along.

Do you feel an urge to pray for others, organizations, schools, businesses, or even the nation and its leaders? If so, prayer and intercession may be your thing.

There are so many ways to do it; just pray.

You will not regret spending time with the Lord. Look at it as if you're having coffee and reading a book with a friend. If you picture Jesus as a friend and your quiet time as a hangout session, you will enjoy your time with Him. Do your thing and rock your very own, unique quiet time.

HIS MERCIES ARE NEW EVERY MORNING

The steadfast love of the LORD never ceases; his mercies never come to an end; they are new every morning; great is your faithfulness.
—LAMENTATIONS 3:22–23, ESV

The Bible says in Mark 1:35, "Very early in the morning, while it was still dark, Jesus got up, left the house and went off to a solitary place, where he prayed" (NIV).

Jesus got up at dark and went off to be alone with the Father. Giving the Lord the first of your day is a wonderful way to start your day. But God's mercy for you does not come only when you spend time with Him in the morning. God's mercy for you starts fresh every single day. Every day is another day to try again, to grow your relationship with Jesus more. But God will bless your time, anytime of day.

If you want to get up early before everyone else, when the house is quiet, and spend time with the Father, go for it. But do not put pressure on yourself to do so. The Lord wants to spend time with you. He wants a relationship with you. If you get up when it is still dark because you like to, then this is a good idea for you. Start your day with the Lord early.

If you get up while it is still dark, open your Bible, and fall asleep for three hours, miss your classes, or arrive late to work, early may not be the best time for you. Remember, Jesus didn't have kids to get up and get ready for school. He didn't have an infant who woke up for feedings three times a night. He didn't have to commute to work, clock in, or get His pay docked for being late.

Any time you can spend with Him is quality time. Even if all you can do when you get out of bed is say, "This is the day the LORD has made; we will rejoice and be glad in it" (Ps. 118:24), or, "Good morning, Lord, I need You today." Just give Him your day. Give Him you.

When the time is right for you, remove yourself from everything else that pulls at your time. If you are a mother with babies at home, your time will be different from a mother whose kids are grown. Turn off all your devices, or put them out of the way; have no distractions. Text your parents or spouse, and say, "I'm spending time with the Lord; call only if it's an emergency." Then, silence that sucker, and put it out of sight. Your mind will wonder and remind you of all the things you need to do. Make notes in your journal, and quiet your mind and your spirit.

There are many different ways to go about spending time with the Lord. I have collected a list of ideas. These are *not* rules, just a few things to ignite your heart and get you to a place that allows you to enjoy your time with the Lord. Do them all, one, or none. I don't care. These are just ideas that I have tried that will help get you started.

Here are some suggestions:

- Pick a time that works for you, even if it's different each day.
- Pick a quiet place that works for you.
- Find a Bible translation you enjoy and understand.
- Grab a journal and a pen—you may want to write your prayers, your dreams, or what you hear the Father saying during your "talk time."

- Play worship music to enter into His presence.
- Pray.
- Listen.
- Read your Bible.
- Pray some more. Listen some more.
- Enjoy your time, and develop your relationship with your friend Jesus.

If Jesus needed time with the Father, it *is* a good plan for you too. The Bible tells us in Jeremiah 33:3, "Call to me and I will answer you and tell you great and unsearchable things you do not know." Basically, when you seek the Lord, you will find Him. When you are quiet and still in His presence, He will show you things you do not know.

Make a plan that works for you.

Talk to Him; then, wait on Him to talk to you.

He might just share some treasures with you about His plans for you.

Once you learn how to enter into His presence and find your place with Him, you will desire to do it more. In your time with Him, He will show you all kinds of wonderful things. You will learn how to apply scripture, understand scripture, and see Him move in amazing ways. Prayer is important and worth every minute. If you don't believe me, ask Jesus; He did it quite often.

17

PRAYER IS ABOUT TRUST

*I*F I ASKED you to raise your hand if you've ever had trust issues, you would drop your book. There is not a person I know who hasn't had someone do them wrong. When this happens, it makes us unsure about trusting the next person.

The whole purpose of this book is to show you the importance of prayer, how prayer is described and used in the Bible. What does it mean to have a quiet time, and why is it important for you?

Part of the reason prayer is so important is that it is how you build a relationship with your heavenly Father. God has called you to be His child. In order to grow in trust with Him, we must have faith.

Like any child, we have to learn we can trust God. Anyone who has a toddler knows they have to learn to trust their parents. Many of us have jumped off the side of the pool or the couch to a parent, trusting they will catch us. We trust we won't be hurt or scared when they are around.

A parent is someone we depend on. When we are near them, we feel secure. If a storm wakes you up in the night, the parents' bed is the place you run to as a child. It is the same way with us when it comes to God—He is our heavenly Father. He is someone we can trust. He is someone we can run to.

All He asks of us is for us to have childlike faith. In Matthew 18:2-4 Jesus called a child to Him and said to those listening, "Truly I tell you, unless you change and become like little children, you will never enter the kingdom of heaven. Therefore, whoever takes the lowly position of this child is the greatest in the kingdom of heaven" (NIV).

As His children, we can ask Him dumb questions, run to Him when we are scared. We can come to Him when we don't know what to do or what to say, and He will let us crawl up in His lap and feel secure.

First John 3:1 says, "What great love the Father has lavished on us, that we should be called children of God! And that is what we are!" (NIV). God calls you His own. He calls you His child. He wants you to put your trust in Him.

How do we put our trust in God?

The first thing to do is accept Jesus as your Lord and Savior through salvation. *If* you have gotten this far in the book and have not done that, stop now and do so. It's simple. I have added a simple prayer here that you can repeat out loud or in your mind, and the work is done.

"God, I admit that I am a sinner in need of a Savior. I submit my life to You and ask You to be my Lord and Savior. Forgive me for trying to do it all without You. I am ready to trust You with my life."

Welcome to the kingdom of God!

> "TRUST IN THE LORD WITH ALL YOUR HEART, AND LEAN NOT ON YOUR OWN UNDERSTANDING; IN ALL YOUR WAYS ACKNOWLEDGE HIM, AND HE SHALL DIRECT YOUR PATHS" (PROV. 3:5-6).

It's a wonderful place full of love. The next thing you need to do is find a Bible and a Bible-preaching church. Both will help you tremendously. And if you have a friend who is a Christian, or a believer, tell them what you just did. They will rejoice with you in your decision.

Now, let's get back to it. How do we put our trust in God?

For some people trust is an issue. You may not have had parents like I described. If this is you, let me be the first to say

I am so sorry you didn't feel as though you could trust your parent(s). Hurt people hurt people. Most of the time they just don't know any better because they did the best they could with what they had. They may not have been loved well and didn't know how to love well.

We can only give what we have gotten. If we have never felt love, we don't know how to love well. If we have never felt as if we were safe with our parents, we may not know how to show that to our children. If this happened to you, I am sorry.

I pray for your heart. If you need to, stop and take a minute to ask God to help you forgive them. You do not have to carry that anymore. You can lay that down and be free from that. Jesus is the perfect person to take this burden from you.

Your parents' failure does not determine your parenting. Your ability to trust your parents does not have to affect you anymore. You can be better. You can be trustworthy. You are called to something different, and today is the day to start new.

Today is the day you grow in trust. Lay down your hurts. Look at what the Lord says in Proverbs 3:5–6: "Trust in the LORD with all your heart, and lean not on your own understanding; in all your ways acknowledge Him, and He shall direct your paths."

Jesus just wants us to trust Him. We cannot rely on what we know and understand. We cannot rely on what we were taught or what we have seen. We cannot rely on anything done or given to you by man. Man will fail you; Jesus will not.

We have to step out and trust the Lord to do something different. In you. In your life. In those around you.

Trust is defined as the "firm belief in the reliability, truth, ability, or strength of someone or something."[1]

Trust is believing that maybe, just maybe, God, the Creator of the universe, has the ability to do a good job controlling your life, believing He has the strength to handle you and that He is reliable.

If no one else has been reliable, give God a chance. He may even help teach you how to be reliable. Or even teach those who caused you to mistrust everyone else how to be reliable.

Trust is not easy, y'all. I know. I still struggle. I let go of stuff and give it to Him and pick it right back up. What I don't realize each time is that I'm not in control anyway; I just think I am.

Building trust in Jesus is done by giving Him a little at a time. Trust Him with something small, and see Him work; then give Him something else. Or, go all in and let Him have it all, and see what happens.

Trust is an unlearning. Trust is letting go of control. Trust is believing that if you manage to let it go, God has the power to help you.

Think of it this way: Your car is making a weird sound, and you take it to the mechanic and let him see what's going on. He finds the problem and fixes it. You could not have found it yourself because you are not a mechanic and haven't had the training. But he did because he knew what he was doing. Do you get the picture?

God knows what He is doing. All you must do is trust Him. The greatest way to grow in trusting the Lord is to start in prayer. When you pray, you learn to talk to God. You grow your relationship with Him. Prayer allows you to tell Him about stuff and trust He is listening; it's learning to trust that He will take care of the situations you talk to Him about.

Prayer is trusting God is transforming who you were into who you are meant to be. Prayer is giving control over to God one request at a time. Prayer is learning to talk to God as a friend. Prayer is talking and listening. Prayer is the fastest way to grow your trust in God.

18

PRAYER IS A BATTLEFIELD

THE ARMOR OF God is one of my all-time favorite things in the Bible, probably because my mom taught it to me as a little girl. We would pray every single day on the way to school like we were physically putting the armor on our bodies. When she said helmet of salvation, we touched our heads and repeated her words. My sister and I were so small, yet the memory is burned in my brain.

She taught it to us from top to bottom. It's not in the same order as the Bible verse, but it made sense to our little-girl minds. It made such an impact I prayed it over my boys when they were small and still pray it over myself.

The Bible version is found in Ephesians 6:10–18 (NIV):

> Finally, be strong in the Lord and in his mighty power. Put on the full armor of God, so that you can take your stand against the devil's schemes. For our struggle is not against flesh and blood, but against the rulers, against the authorities, against the powers of this dark world and against the spiritual forces of evil in the heavenly realms. Therefore put on the full armor of God, so that when the day of evil comes, you may be able to stand your ground, and after you have done everything, to stand. Stand firm then, with the belt of truth buckled around your waist, with the breastplate of righteousness in place, and with your feet fitted with the readiness that comes from the gospel of peace. In addition to all this, take up the shield of faith, with which you can extinguish all the flaming arrows of the evil one. Take the

helmet of salvation and the sword of the Spirit, which is the word of God. And pray in the Spirit on all occasions with all kinds of prayers and requests. With this in mind, be alert and always keep on praying for all the Lord's people.

The parts of the armor of God in order are the belt of truth, the breastplate of righteousness, shoes of the gospel of peace, the shield of faith, the helmet of salvation, and the sword of the Spirit.

Priscilla Shirer has an incredible Bible study on the armor of God and goes into more depth on the importance of each piece and the order. The way I learned it was from head to toe. It made sense in my mind, and I have always done it this way. I will share the prayer, and you can take it as your own, or come up with one that follows the proper biblical order.

Feel free to physically touch your body in these spots to represent dressing yourself in God's armor.

> *I put on the armor of God with the helmet of salvation, the breastplate of righteousness; I guard my loins with the belt of truth. My feet have on the shoes of the gospel of peace. I hold in my right hand the sword of the Spirit and in my left hand the shield of faith so that I may quench the fiery darts of the wicked one.*

OK, now you are dressed for battle.

Why is this so important?

I have listed the full section of Scripture for reference.

Just before the Bible goes into the armor of God, Paul says in verse 10, "Finally, be strong in the Lord and in his mighty power" (NIV). The armor of God covers us with the attributes of God. This is some powerful, next-level stuff here.

I am going to show this to you in my head-to-toe order because it makes sense to me this way.

Here goes:

Helmet of salvation—protects and covers my mind from negative thoughts or selfish thoughts of how *I've* got this and need no one else. Wrong, you need God's help to fight Satan, period. Your salvation is your saving grace. Salvation gives you a seat at God's table. It is God saving you from sin. It is God becoming your partner in life so you can walk in step with Him and have an abundant life through Christ.

Salvation changes your position. You are no longer a slave to sin but a surrendered follower of Christ. Salvation renames you chosen, forgiven, adopted, and accepted. It changes your thinking to the mind of Christ. This helmet covers your brain and replaces your thinking with God's thinking. The helmet is not to be left. It is a key piece of battle-wear. Without it you doubt yourself and continue on in fear that you don't have what it takes and aren't strong enough.

Well, you are right, you aren't. But God in you and with you is strong enough. Remember, we are to be strong in the Lord and *His* mighty power.

Breastplate of righteousness—protects all your main organs. This is similar to a police vest. It covers the front and back and protects your organs from assault. Not only that, but it covers your heart. Your heart will lead you astray, but when you are in your armor, it is covered by the blood of Jesus and His righteousness.

Righteousness is not something we can earn. It is a free gift at salvation. It is a process of right living. But it is not something we can get on our own. When Jesus died on the cross a sinless Lamb, He took our sin and nailed it to the cross. He paid our account in full. He stripped us of our worthlessness and covered us in His righteousness.

The breastplate is a bulletproof vest we get from God to guard our hearts and organs from the enemy's attack. Don't leave this one at home either.

Belt of truth—Guard my loins with the belt of truth. This is the belt that holds it all together. Jesus is "the way, the truth, and the life" (John 14:6). This belt is like wrapping yourself up in who He says you are, not what the world says.

Most belts aren't super important, but this one is. Belts are cute, but they also hold your pants up. This belt holds the breastplate and covers the private area.

When I was a kid, I had no clue what loins were. Now I do, and I think it's interesting that God has an armor piece to protect that spot. Why? Because He calls us to "be fruitful and multiply" in Genesis 1:28. He is strategic in how He wants us to do that as well. He wants us to believe the truth about this area. It is not for display but for your spouse. He wants our entire body wrapped in the truth of who He says we are, and He starts the whole section here.

He is a God of order. His order in this matters. I learned it out of order and didn't realize until later the significance of the belt being first. Truth is the most important. Once we learn the truth, who He is, then we learn who we are as His children. The belt is not to be left behind. It is the first thing to put on because it holds all the rest of it together.

Feet shod with preparation of the **gospel of peace**—My mom taught me this one, and I would put it on like a pair of shoes. Picture each step being a step of peace. Fear has to leave when you take each step on a shoe of peace.

Imagine a soldier walking for hours on all kinds of terrain, possibly even sleeping standing up, if they get to sleep. When a battle is raging, sometimes there is no stopping to rest. Commercials sell these shoes that are squishy and comfortable, but these shoes are walking on God's peace. Sign me up for seven pairs, please.

Sword of the Spirit—This is the Word of God. The Bible tells us to hide God's Word in our hearts in several spots. Here are two:

Psalm 119:11: "Thy word have I hid in mine heart, that I might not sin against thee" (KJV).

Psalm 37:31: "The law of his God is in his heart; none of his steps shall slide." In just these two references, hiding God's Word, memorizing, believing, and following the Word of God, does two things: (1) it keeps you from sin, and (2) it keeps your feet from slipping.

The Word of God is powerful! Hebrews 4:12 says, "For the word of God is alive and active. Sharper than any double-edged sword, it penetrates even to dividing soul and spirit, joints and marrow; it judges the thoughts and attitudes of the heart" (NIV).

The Word of God is a weapon. In the armor of God it is a sword. God's Word is like a double-edged sword and can be used for your protection to fight off the enemy. The more you know it, the stronger you are. Using God's Word in prayer is using already anointed words. God's word is a game changer. The sword is the only offensive weapon in your armor; it is substantial. Do not—I repeat, do not—leave your sword at home.

Shield of faith—This is the protection extraordinaire. Ephesians literally follows the shield of faith with these words, "with which you can extinguish all the flaming arrows of the evil one" (NIV). What?

In this war, Satan and his demons are shooting flaming arrows at you—not just arrows, flaming arrows. Your only defense is your shield. Your shield protects you from getting hit. It is your main defense. You cannot move forward without this shield.

What kind of shield is it? A shield of *faith*. Your faith in God is what runs this whole thing, your faith to choose to follow Him and be saved. Enter salvation and the helmet. Your faith to choose to walk away from a life of sin, enter the righteousness of Jesus and your breastplate. Your faith to believe that God, Jesus, and the Holy Spirit are real and choose to follow them, enter truth and the belt that holds it all together.

All your armor is based on your faith. Your salvation and life are based on your faith. The Bible says earlier, in Ephesians 2:8–9, "For it is by grace you have been saved, through faith—and this is not from yourselves, it is the gift of God—not by works, so that no one can boast" (NIV).

God, in His gracious mercy and love, chose to give His only Son, Jesus to die for you (John 3:16). By faith you chose to believe and follow Him and take Him as your Savior. This choice gives you the right to be called a child of God, to earn His righteousness and learn to walk in the peace of God that transcends all our earthly minds' understanding. God is way beyond us. But He chooses us every single day.

Your faith in Him gives you all-access, backstage passes to the armor of God.

Wow! You and I are so unworthy and undeserving of any of this. *But God.* He freely gives when we don't deserve it.

What is the purpose of this armor?

> Put on the full armor of God, so that you can take your stand against the devil's schemes. For our struggle is not against flesh and blood, but against the rulers, against the authorities, against the powers of this dark world and against the spiritual forces of evil in the heavenly realms.
>
> —vv. 11–12, NIV

We are fighting the devil. I mentioned this already, but this guy is violent and without remorse. First Peter 5:8 says, "Be sober, be vigilant; because *your* adversary the devil walks about like a roaring lion, seeking whom he may devour" (emphasis added).

Not me. Not you. Satan has no authority but the power we give him. When we are equipped with the armor of God, we are ready for battle.

Ephesians warns us in verse 12 that the battle is not against flesh and blood but rulers and authorities and powers of darkness and spiritual forces of evil.

Back the truck up. That is scary.

I don't know how to battle powers of darkness and spiritual forces.

SATAN HAS NO AUTHORITY BUT THE POWER WE GIVE HIM. WHEN WE ARE EQUIPPED WITH THE ARMOR OF GOD, WE ARE READY FOR BATTLE.

No—but God does.

When we put on God's armor, we are getting all His attributes. We are covered from head to toe. We have a sword and a shield. We have His word hidden in our hearts. We are clothed in salvation, righteousness, and truth. We are walking in the peace of God. We are using God's Word as a weapon of spiritual warfare. And we are covered from the flaming arrows by the shield of faith.

Fear is not an option. Faith is. Peace is. Strength is.

Remember where we started—be strong in the Lord and His mighty power.

Check. When I am in my own armor, I am weak. When I am clothed in His armor, I am strong in His strength and mighty power.

Now for my favorite part.

> Therefore put on the full armor of God, so that when the day of evil comes, you may be able to stand your

ground, and after you have done everything, to stand. Stand firm then.

—vv. 13–14, NIV

Soldier, here are your orders:

Put on the armor of God.

Wait for evil to come (because it will).

Stand your ground.

Do everything to stand.

Stand firm then.

My favorite part is, stand. When having done all to stand, stand firm then.

This part gets me pumped like listening to a *Rocky* song before a football game. I can see a wavering and weary warrior slowing down after a hard-fought battle, staggering to hide for a minute to just catch his breath and check his wounds. He wants to lie down and go home and rest, but he can't. His commander said to hold the line. He is being asked to stay standing, sword in hand, heavy armor weighing him down, and a shield to keep him from dying.

The warrior wavers and staggers, but he renews his mind, takes a deep breath, straightens up, adjusts his gear, checks his weapon, and stands. Though he is exhausted and it is all he has in him to not fall down, he stands firm then.

You are the warrior.

This battle is not yours to fight alone, but you are fighting in the army of God. You are wearing His armor, using His weapons, guarded by your faith in Him. You are in a battle of spiritual warfare.

> "No weapon formed against you shall prosper, and every tongue which rises against you in judgment you shall condemn. This is the heritage of the servants of the LORD, and their righteousness is from Me," says the LORD.
>
> —ISAIAH 54:17

Lastly, let's look at Ephesians 6:18: "And pray in the Spirit on all occasions with all kinds of prayers and requests. With this in mind, be alert and always keep on praying for all the Lord's people" (NIV). Read the full chapter.

Pray. Every single battle that is won is done on your knees. You don't have to physically be on your knees; just pray. The world is pushing its agenda hard. The only way to withstand it is to pray. Put on your armor, trust God is with you, and pray.

Ephesians tells us how to armor up. Then it says to stand firm when it is so hard you want to give up. Then it says to pray. Pray in the Spirit, with all kinds of prayer and supplication.

James 5:16 says, "The prayer of a righteous person is powerful and effective" (NIV).

Your prayers are powerful, mighty warrior. Trust God. Trust God in you. Put on your armor and pray.

TYPES OF PRAYER

PRAYER OF FAITH

Faith is the substance of things hoped for, the evidence of things not seen.

—HEBREWS 11:1

*P*RAYER IS FAITH, and faith is praying. When we pray, we are believing for something, not knowing if we will get it but hoping it happens. Prayer is believing God will do something to change the situation. Faith is defined as complete confidence and trust in someone or something.

You can go back and read James 5:13–16 as I broke it down in the prayer-for-healing section in chapter 13. Prayer actually grows our faith. Sometimes it is easier to believe for another person than it is to believe for yourself. When you pray for other people and grow your faith, it becomes easier to believe for yourself. We develop an "If God will do it for them, He will do it for me" mindset.

Every time we talk to God through prayer, it is another connection point. The more we get to know Him, the more we trust Him. Similarly to all your other friendships, the conversation grows the depth of the relationship. If you want big faith, pray.

There's a story in Matthew 9:14–29 about a little boy with an unclean spirit. The boy's father had tried everything to no avail. Then he encountered Jesus and the disciples. They brought the father to Jesus. Jesus spoke to the father in Mark 9:22–24.

The boy's father: "If You can do anything, have compassion on us and help us" (v. 22).

Jesus: "If you can believe, all things are possible to him who believes" (v. 23).

The boy's father: "Lord, I believe; help my unbelief" (v. 24).

You may be believing in a financial breakthrough or a prodigal child. You cannot see anything changing and are trying to trust God with the impossible. You may need to trust God for healing for a child or a bleak diagnosis. Ask God to help you with your unbelief.

Search for the word *faith* in the Bible, and start memorizing those verses. Pray those verses, and insert your name. Pray for yourself, and believe for faith for yourself. But most importantly, believe God is who He says He is.

Play worship music and worship your way to faith. Claim what the Word says and the words of the songs. Ask God for the gift of faith. It is free.

PRAYER OF REPENTANCE

To repent is to ask for forgiveness, or express remorse. Basically, it's an apology. Your first prayer of repentance is when you pray and ask Jesus into your heart at salvation. You admit you are a sinner in need of a Savior and forgiveness, and accept Him as your Savior. Forgiveness comes, and if you are in a church or around other believers, you learn how to stop what you were doing and change your ways.

Although you will still mess up because you are human, this is the basic idea of salvation. As you learn how to follow Jesus, you learn to let go of your past and live a life that represents Jesus well. As a parent, when you have your kids apologize to each other, you are teaching them to see the error of their ways, learn to be kind, and admit when they are wrong. It's basic parenting but basic Christianity as well. As a parent you also learn to apologize for your own mistakes, if you yell, get them to school late, throw away something they wanted, and so on. Again, they learn by watching you. If you admit you are wrong and ask for forgiveness, they will learn to do the same.

One thing about asking for forgiveness and saying you're sorry that goes unchecked is, if you are really sorry, you should change. Let that marinate.

Most of the time we say we're sorry about a mean joke that hurt someone's feelings, we end up doing it over and over again and act as if saying we're sorry makes it OK. It doesn't. It still hurts the person. When you do it over and over and it becomes a habit, it hurts them and you. This is the same for sin. It hurts us, it hurts God, and it hurts the other person involved.

Many people think if they asked for forgiveness once and got saved, they're good. Well, you may be. God is a super gracious God. But does that hurt you to just get away with it over and over and not have remorse or a sorrowful heart about your repetitive sin? If you are doing something over and over and don't feel sorry for it, you may ought to check your heart status.

If you are doing something over and over and have regret and conviction, you know in your heart it is wrong. The Bible says in James 4:17, "To him who knows to do good and does not do it, to him it is sin." If you get a gut feeling of, "Shoot, I did it again," it is time to say a prayer of repentance. As for forgiveness. Say you are sorry. Give it to the Lord and trust Him to help you. Do it as much as you need. He is our helper. He knows what you are doing even if you won't admit it. Once you do, you shine a light on the sin and Satan loses the power over you.

Ephesians 5:11 says, "Do not have fellowship with the unfruitful works of darkness; instead, expose them" (MEV). Verse 13 says, "All things are exposed when they are revealed by the light, for everything that becomes visible is light" (MEV).

Jesus is the light of the world. The world is full of darkness, and when we behave like the world, we allow darkness to enter. Once we admit our sin and ask for forgiveness, we expose it to the light. Sin and Satan lose their power.

Ephesians 5:8–9 says, "For you were formerly darkness [unsaved], but now you are light in the Lord. Walk as children of light—for the fruit of the Spirit is in all goodness and righteousness and truth" (MEV). The truth is Jesus. And we need the truth every single day to help us live in this world and not be of this world. If we learn to live a repentant lifestyle through prayer, we will always be peaceful when we close our eyes at night. Keeping a short account of our issues keeps us in contact with Jesus and living in the light, as He is the light.

Darkness and sin do not have your heart; Jesus does. Don't let them get the best of you. When Jesus came to the attempted stoning with the woman caught in adultery, he said, "Neither do I condemn you; go and sin no more" (John 8:11). Jesus knows we are not perfect; only He was. He doesn't expect perfection. His whole purpose is forgiveness.

Paul tells us in Romans 8:1, "There is therefore now no condemnation to those who are in Christ Jesus." When we come to Jesus with repentant hearts, He says to us as He did the woman, "I do not condemn you; go and sin no more."

If you need this prayer, do not delay. It will bring you freedom to ask for forgiveness and find it in the name of Jesus.

PRAYER OF LAMENT

One of the most well-known people in the Bible, other than Jesus of course, is King David. Many books have been written about him, and he is the man the Bible calls "a man after [God's] own heart" (Acts 13:22).

> You can't know joy until you have known sorrow.
> —ANNE WITH AN E

You can't understand the depths of love until you have felt the pain of losing it. I think a guy named Kahlil Gibran says this with a bit more eloquence. But my wording makes sense to me.

Mark Twain said, "What is joy without sorrow? What is success without failure? What is a win without a loss? What is health without illness? You have to experience each if you are to appreciate the other. There is always going to be suffering. It's how you look at your suffering, how you deal with it, that will define you."[1]

Lament is such a real thing there is an entire book in the Bible that is a lament—it is called Lamentations. We see prayers of lament from Job, Habakkuk, and King David in Psalms.

A lament is a passionate expression of grief or sorrow; to lament is to mourn. When we lament, we are basically in agony over a situation and asking God to intervene. It's almost as if we're begging from a place of deep grief and desperation. Lamenting is a place where we can go but should not stay.

Don't build your house on Lament Street.

Years ago the Lord showed me that I had become so familiar with the place we had been in our lives that I had fallen down and settled there. I had staked my claim in that spot, and even if He wanted to move me, it was as if I were stuck in the ground there. Sometimes our valleys last for so long they seem to become who we are, not just where we are. Then they become where we stay.

The Father showed me on the ground, stuck in sorrow, frustration, familiarity, despondency, and inadequacy. He said, "Get up." He didn't want me to get stuck there. He had more for me, and all I had to do was brush off the familiar place and be OK with packing my bags and going.

Sometimes we become so familiar with a wound, or a fear, or a sickness, or pain, we forget that we aren't called to stay there. We are called to get up. We are called to believe for more. Don't settle in a place where He hasn't put you. Pour out your frustrations, hurts, and sorrows to God, and let them go. Get up, dust it off, and take another step.

We must lament to move forward. We have to lay down our fears, mistakes, and concerns. We must weep over our sin or sin within our family so we can pour it out at the feet of Jesus. Then we must leave it there.

God's Holy Spirit gives us tears to let it out. After our cry we can recalibrate. We ask for forgiveness for ourselves. We forgive those who hurt us. Then we receive the tender loving mercies the Father hands out and press on.

Now it is time to remember your dreams and desires. Forget what happened, and believe for a better future. Remember our God who saves, heals, delivers, and sets free. Get up. Wipe your tears. Straighten your shirt and stand tall. Don't build your house on Lament Street. This was only a visit. You were never meant to dwell there.

PRAYER OF BLESSING

When I think of a prayer of blessing, I think about all the verses I know that are the promises of God. I want to add them into a long paragraph and say, "Bring it, Lord." I also think about this random guy's prayer, tucked in the Old Testament where no one expects to come across it. The prayer of Jabez is tucked in the middle of a list of lineage names in 1 Chronicles 4:10: "Jabez called on the God of Israel saying, 'Oh, that You would bless me indeed, and enlarge my territory, that Your hand would be with me, and that You would keep me from evil, that I may not cause pain!' So God granted him what he requested."

During the lineage of David and the line of Judah sits a guy named Jabez. Verse 9 says Jabez was more honorable than his brothers but born into hardship. He was named in regard to hardship. Hardship was his identity and destiny, and Jabez thought, "No, I don't want to stay there." Jabez prayed a prayer asking God for a couple of things:

- Bless me, Lord.
- Enlarge my territory.
- God, be with me.
- Keep me from evil.
- Don't bring me pain.

He basically asked God to circumvent his identity and change it. He must have known and believed God could do exceedingly, abundantly more than he could ask or imagine. Based on the little we know, he was not destined for an easy life of God's provision, blessing, protection, and salvation from harm. Talk about faith. He saw outside of his life into the heart of a God who loved him, and asked for his personal needs to be met. It was as easy as that. He just believed and asked, and God granted his request.

Think about your personal needs you'd like met from a God who loves you and knows you. Start with the prayer of Jabez, and see where it leads. God is not a genie, but He is a loving, providing, protecting God. I mean, what could it hurt?

Prayer for Wisdom, Righteousness

When I first started reading the Bible, I started in Proverbs. It has thirty-one chapters, one for each day of the month. I mean, it is the book of wisdom; of course it has one chapter per day. Isn't it amazing how God knew when He spoke the words through the author Solomon that we could use a spot to start that gave us a good daily guide?

One of the things I love about Proverbs is the contrast between the righteous and the wicked. It gives pointers about what the Lord says about the righteous, then about the wicked. It's a back-and-forth contrast between the two.

Read Proverbs and see where you find yourself. Do you fit on the wicked list, or the righteous list? You may have to do a prayer of repentance for some things, but the more we are with Him, in His Word, and in prayer, the more we grow in righteousness.

We will never be perfect. God doesn't expect perfect; He just wants you. So be a Solomon today and ask for wisdom. Begin to pray it over yourself, your spouse, and your kids. What better gift can you give the people you love than prayers for God to bless them with His wisdom!

Start with this: "God, thank You for giving me godly wisdom. Help me see myself as You see me. Give me an understanding of Your Word and Your plan for me. Grow me in wisdom, knowledge, and understanding so my life will reflect Your righteousness. Thank You. Amen."

PRAYER OF SUPPLICATION

Supplication is a petition for something—when you ask for something, when you beg for something, when you present a request for a need or want, pleading with God in prayer.

I have personally done this many times when I was suffering with a migraine, or watching one of the kids suffer in pain or sickness. This type of prayer could also be seen in a hospital room or chapel. Some people fall to their knees in humility as if they realize they are beneath the One whom they are petitioning. This represents a sincere request.

This prayer may include thanksgiving but is truly a petition, possibly even reminding God of what He promises in His Word and requesting for Him to perform it for their situation.

One of the most well-known verses including supplication explains this prayer. Philippians 4:6 says, "Be anxious for nothing, but in everything by prayer and supplication, with thanksgiving, let your requests be made known to God." My breakdown: Pray about everything without being anxious, thank God, and tell Him all your troubles.

This is another way the Bible shows us how to pray. The following verse gives us an if-then statement of what happens when we do it this way. If we pray this way, then:

Philippians 4:7 says, "And the peace of God, which transcends all understanding, will guard your hearts and your minds in Christ Jesus" (NIV).

Hello, my hand is raised here. Sign me up for peace in my heart and mind that is beyond my understanding. Yes, please!

Psalm 6:9 says, "The LORD has heard my supplication; the LORD will receive my prayer."

In my opinion, this is the kind of prayer Hannah prayed. She petitioned God so intensely that the priest thought she was drunk. She was begging God for a son. He promised to give her one if she would give him back to God. Even in her barrenness she trusted God.

After God answered her prayer and the boy was weaned, she took him to the temple and gave him back to the Lord. His name was Samuel. Once she left him, she prayed again. This time she exalted who the Lord is and fully put her trust in Him even though she didn't know God's plan for her son. She gave up her son because she promised him to the Lord; then she walked away in full trust.

She prayed two different types of prayer. Hannah is a great example of praying in all circumstances and offering God unwavering devotion regardless of the circumstance. She fully trusted God in each scenario.

PRAYER OF TRAVAIL

Travail is something that is painful and laborious, possibly a plea for a loved one during a life-threatening illness, accident, or surgery. This is a gut-wrenching prayer from a place of pain, hurt, and possibly fear.

Sometimes people say, "You must travail before you prevail." I heard that when I was a little girl in my grandfather's church. I'm not sure this terminology is used anymore. Travail is similar to a lament because it is a heart's cry.

As a mother, I would say this type of prayer was used by Sarai, the wife of Abraham, when she was begging God for a child as He promised, possibly even when she was heartbroken Abram had a child with Hagar and she was jealous and hateful, and then again when Abraham took Isaac up the mountain for a sacrifice and took no sacrifice. I am almost positive her mother's heart had a gut check at that moment.

I can hear her calling out to Abraham and Isaac as he walked off, "Honey, don't forget the lamb or the goat. Honey, do you hear me?" As they walk away, she travails to God in utter anguish. "Oh, my God, Father of creation, You promised me Isaac, and we waited so long. Please, Yahweh, do not let my lord (Abraham) harm my son of the promise." Then, because she is a woman, her mind wanders and fear grips her, and she prays fervently until both of them return weeks later.

I'm sure in the same way, Hagar travailed when she believed her and Ishmael would die in the desert. Then God, El Roi, showed up.

It's my opinion, but I believe this is what *travail* means. I have been in this place for my loved ones who were sick unto death, begging God to spare them and heal them.

Psalm 5:2 says, "Give heed to the voice of my cry, my King and my God, for to You I will pray."

Micah 4:10 says, "Be in pain, and labor to bring forth, O daughter of Zion, like a woman in birth pangs. For now you shall go forth from the city, you shall dwell in the field, and to Babylon you shall go. There you shall be delivered; there the LORD will redeem you from the hand of your enemies."

Psalm 25:18 says, "Consider mine affliction and my travail; and forgive all my sins" (ASV).

Travail is mentioned about thirty times in the Bible, mostly with the term "like a woman in travail." So, it must be something a woman does when she is groaning from her insides. This is the cry of a mother's heart.

Being a mother is unique. You can be an incredible nanny, but once you have a child, your entire perspective changes. Things that never crossed your mind before become larger than life. You begin to see harmful things and recognize things you missed before.

I have begged God from the depths of my soul for my sons to get well when they are sick, for my sons to resist temptation and a life of sin. I have prayed for their health, salvation, friends, choices, college, jobs, and even wives. I have even prayed a few friends and girls out of their lives.

There is a deep groaning that occurs when you are begging God for the health and safety of your son or daughter. Suffice to say, your momma may have prayed this way for you; I know mine did.

I was about nineteen when my mom called me on the phone to check on me. I was walking down a four-lane highway alone at night when she called. She had no idea what I was doing or where I was, but the Holy Spirit did. He warned her, and she was travailing for me. She prayed, felt the nudging of the Holy Spirit, and then she called me because she was concerned for my safety. She was correct. I was walking alone at night on a highway because I was safer walking than I was in the car with my boyfriend at the time. He was abusive, and she knew something was wrong, but I wouldn't admit it. I escaped the car and took off walking to get away.

Her gut-wrenching, deep-in-her-soul cry to the Lord possibly forced me from the car and gave her the urge to call me. She came and picked me up and talked to me the entire way. I found my way to a store and waited for her. The Holy Spirit was my mother's lifeline to God for me. The Holy Spirit was also my Savior many times.

The deep cry of your heart for your children, your spouse, your parents, and your siblings is real. Cry out to God. Give it to Him and trust Him with it. When you get woken up at night to pray, do it. When you get a call to pray, do it. A mother's instinct is no joke. God gave you the motherly side of His heart when He created you. Trust God's gut in you.

PRAYER OF THANKSGIVING

One of the things we should do most when we praise is thank the Lord for all He has done for us that we don't deserve. We deserve death, but Jesus paid it all. We should enter every time of prayer revering His holy name and thanking Him for all He does for us.

This reminds me of a song from my childhood called "He Has Made Me Glad," about thanksgiving. This entire song is from the Bible verses in Psalm 100. Verse 4 says, "Enter his gates with thanksgiving and his courts with praise" (NIV). Psalm 118:24 says, "This is the day the LORD has made; we will rejoice and be glad in it."

If we would learn to be thankful first, we might shift our perspective toward the Father. All our problems seem a little smaller in the big scheme of things. We may even find what we lack is not so bad after all.

First Thessalonians 5:16–18 says, "Rejoice always, pray

without ceasing, in everything give thanks; for this is the will of God in Christ Jesus for you."

Colossians 4:2 says, "Devote yourselves to prayer, being watchful and thankful" (NIV).

THANKFULNESS SHIFTS OUR COMPLAINING AND LETS US SEE THE THINGS TO BE GRATEFUL FOR. THEN OUR FAITH GROWS AND OUR COMPLAINTS AND PROBLEMS FEEL LESS HARD.

Apparently, God knows we need to pray, and when we do, we should be thankful. In the midst of all the things life throws at you, some days it is hard to find one thing to be thankful for. Here's a guarantee: When you start to count your blessings, you will discover how many there are.

If we would enter into prayer appreciating God for our gifts, our perspective would drastically shift. Let us remember to thank God every day, every time we pray for our blessings.

"Let us come into his presence with thanksgiving; let us make a joyful noise to him with songs of praise" (Ps. 95:2, ESV).

Not only does God want to hear your thank-you; He wants you to sing praise to His name. Add these two together, and all of a sudden your stress fades and His presence comes near.

Thankfulness shifts our mindset from us to Him. Thankfulness shifts our complaining and lets us see the things to be grateful for. Then our faith grows and our complaints and problems feel less hard. Our strength grows as our faith grows, all from being thankful first.

INTERCESSORY PRAYER

> Therefore I exhort first of all that you make supplications, prayers, intercessions, and thanksgivings for everyone.
>
> —1 TIMOTHY 2:1, MEV

I remember the first time I heard about someone who was an intercessor. There was a lady who walked the halls of the school and touched every locker and prayed for every single kid. An intercessor is someone who prays on behalf of another person.

My mother-in-law, Stevie, was an intercessor. She had unsaved family members she prayed for daily. She prayed for the president, regardless of whether she voted for him. She prayed for her kids and grandkids. She loved spending time with the Lord, and He would call on her to pray for people no one else was praying for.

When I think of intercessory prayer, I recall a time when I thought, "That's just not my thing." Then I went and had kids who became teenagers and would be battling temptation and looking for a godly spouse. I didn't realize in my time of learning to pray and spend time with the Lord that He was building a heart of intercession inside me.

God started it all for me when He asked me to start praying over my house. He wanted me to worship Him first, then move into prayer. Once the boys left for school and Matt went to work, I would ask the Lord for a song and play it loud from my phone or attach it to my television, and start worshipping. When you worship, you set the mood of your spirit to reverence for the Father. All the things that weigh on you heavy begin to lighten up.

During worship I didn't care what I sounded like because to Him it was a joyful noise of His daughter exalting His name. While I magnified His name, He took my cares and sorrows and traded them for peace and joy. He met me there and began to change my heart.

After worship I would move into the three boys' room and pray. Most of the time I would start by thanking the Lord because my heart of worship helped grow my heart of gratitude. As I thanked the Lord, the prayers would flow. Spending the time worshipping Him connected our hearts, and He gave me revelation of what to pray for each boy. I would also move into our room and pray over Matt.

Whether I was praying in English or my prayer language, God always met me there. His presence would settle upon me and invade my prayers. His words would come out as I prayed for my boys and Matt. Every single time, it is a beautiful experience of closeness with Father God, the moments when heaven and earth collide, when His kingdom comes and His will is prayed to be done.

Intercessory, praying for other people, is an honor. When you are called to do it, your heart for the person or situation grows in love. Some are called to pray for people they do not know or know well. Some are called to pray and never tell a soul; just God knows.

Intercession reminds me of pregnancy. Don't let me lose you here. Bear with me; let me explain. The Lord will drop a little seed inside your heart for a person or situation. The Holy Spirit will nudge and remind you of them, and you will lift up a prayer. The nudge will begin to grow, and you won't be able to shake it. This is an intercessory seed.

As the Lord grows the seed to pray for this person or situation, it becomes intense within you. You think about it, dream about it, and constantly pray over it. You dwell in this place of prayer until the burden lifts. When the burden lifts and the pressure to stay in an attitude of constant prayer shifts, it is like you have birthed it and you are done.

My Gram used the term *praying it through*. You pray about it until it's done. You remain consistent until the feeling passes, if you will. You may be praying for someone to be healed or saved, and it may result in healing or salvation. It may also result in the Lord moving you on and someone else to them. You don't always see the answer; you just trust God and the process.

The Bible talks about intercessory prayer in a couple of

places. Let's start with when Jesus interceded for us. You will find this prayer in John 17:1–26. It is too long to add here, but grab your Bible and take a minute when you can. Jesus asks God to do for us as He (God) did for Him (Jesus). In reading this prayer, I can find eight to ten things Jesus asks God to do or give to us. He prays for us just before He is betrayed and sent to be judged and crucified. Jesus' last prayer before it all went down was for God to bless us—such great love.

Also, the Holy Spirit intercedes for us. Paul says in Romans 8:26 (MEV), "Likewise, the Spirit helps us in our weaknesses, for we do not know what to pray for as we ought, but the Spirit Himself intercedes for us with groanings too deep for words." Verse 27 says, "He who searches the hearts knows what the mind of the Spirit is, because He intercedes for the saints according to the will of God" (MEV).

As you continue in Romans 8, it asks who can charge us. When we have Jesus, who died and rose again, there is none to condemn. Verse 34 says, "[Jesus] who is at the right hand of God, who also intercedes for us" (NASB).

Jesus interceded for us before His death and does so in heaven at the right hand of God. Thank you, Jesus; oh, how I long for more of You.

The Holy Spirit has deep, intense prayers of intercession for us that connect us to the will of God. How glorious is that? If the Holy Spirit intercedes for me, I want more of the Holy Spirit and what He has to offer too.

20

OH, THE GLORY OF
HIS PRESENCE

I MENTIONED IN THE previous chapter about the presence of God coming into my home and the boys' rooms when I prayed. Feeling the glory of the Lord is what I mean by His presence. When you do, you will know.

How do I enter into His presence, and what does that mean?

When the song in the previous section mentions entering His gates and His courts, does that mean heaven? What in the world is meant by His presence? I'm not going to court or through a gate. Huh?

I'm glad you asked!

We cannot talk about the presence of the Lord without first mentioning Adam and Eve and how God literally walked and talked with them in the garden of Eden. They were in true fellowship, relationship with God in human form walking along with them. That is some amazing stuff right there.

Then sin happened, and the world started to fall apart. Wickedness happened, but God never left.

Adam and Eve were booted out of the garden, but God continued to commune with them. They were not who God needed for the rest of the story. God was looking for someone who would listen and obey.

God found Noah and led him into a lifesaving building project. Noah obeyed even to the degree of looking like a moron and losing his friends. But his obedience saved his and his family's lives. God made a promise to the world with Noah, the rainbow, His promise to never flood the earth again. This flood was a reboot because the world and its people had fallen so evil.

Later, God called Abram and asked him to step out of his comfort zone and leave his creature comforts to travel around. Abram left home and became a nomad, moved his tent when God told him to, and just trusted. God made promises to Abram about him having generations to follow him. Yet Abram and his wife had no children. Still, they remained faithful and trusted God. Abram was later renamed Abraham (just in case I lost you). A childless man became Father Abraham who had many sons from the children's song. God gave him two, and the legacies of the world came from him.

God made a covenant with Adam, Noah, and Abraham because they obeyed when He asked. They trusted God, and God trusted them. They were nowhere near perfect, but God.

Sin kept rearing its ugly head, people died, towns got burned, but God. He was in the middle, intertwining all the stories. Following Adam, Noah, and Abraham were Isaac, Jacob, and Joseph. They all have incredible stories of what God did in their lives. Joseph, the dreamer, was sold by his brothers and later saved them from death. You can't make this stuff up. The Bible is full of action-packed stories. And all of that I just listed is just in Genesis.

Enter Moses—you know, the baby in the basket. This dude ended up being a total stud leader. Before God called him, he was an abandoned baby who had been adopted into the king's home. He had a half-brother he fought with, some sort of speaking problem, and a heart for the slaves of the land. Moses had a heart God could work with, and so it began.

He was a mess, and a whole generation followed his leadership. His story is in Exodus. He's the guy who first experienced

God's voice in a fire inside a bush that didn't burn up. God called him to be a leader, and he was wigged-out.

He first discovered the presence in the unburned bush, God's voice in the fire.

He later watched God move all around him. Moses and God made a plan to save the Israelite slaves. Moses saw so many miracles during the plagues in Exodus 7–14, and even saw God divide the Red Sea to save a whole nation.

Once Moses got a taste of God, he was hooked. He still had doubt, but when he was asked to do life-threatening things and trust God boldly, he did. God never failed Moses; He just kept showing up. Grab your Bible and meet me in Exodus. Let's dig into the presence of the Lord.

In Exodus 13 God's presence shows up in a wild way. Verse 21 says, "The LORD [Yahweh] went before them by day in a pillar of cloud to lead them along the way, and by night in a pillar of fire, to give them light, so that they might travel by day and by night" (MEV).

Verse 22: "He [God, Yahweh] did not remove the pillar of cloud by day or the pillar of fire by night from before the people" (MEV).

Has your mouth dropped yet? This pillar was the "glory" of the Lord in His full majesty on display for all to see. His presence traveled with them day and night. He protected them day and night. When the pillar moved, the people moved. When the pillar stopped, the people stopped and set up camp.

Moses led the Israelites with a pillar of cloud by day and a pillar of fire by night. Little did he know this was just a glimpse of what God had in store for him. He was about to encounter God's presence like never before.

Moses' journey with God is so huge and incredible. Let's take a look. The Israelites escaped slavery; God promised them a home He called the promised land. He gave them bread and quail from heaven to feed them in the desert. So many other things transpired, and God decided to talk to everyone from a thick cloud and scared the liver out of the people. So, Moses went to meet and talk with God, and he took Aaron, his brother.

In chapter 20 God wrote the Ten Commandments and some other laws. He also spelled out what Moses was to build so the people could worship God. It was pretty detailed but cool to imagine.

In chapter 33 God and Moses had a talk, and this is the part that sets my shoes on fire. Moses had such a hunger to spend time with the Lord he asked to see God's glory in Exodus 33:18.

Here is God's answer from verse 19 (MEV): "I will make all My goodness pass before you, and I will proclaim the name of the LORD before you. I will be gracious to whom I will be gracious and will show mercy on whom I will show mercy." Then God said in verse 20, "You cannot see My face, for no man can see Me and live" (MEV).

In verses 21–23 God explains what He will do. OK, Moses, here's what's up. "Indeed, there is a place by Me. You must stand on the rock. While my glory passes by, I will put you in a cleft of the rock and will cover you with My hand while I pass by. Then I will take away My hand, and you will see My back, but My face may not be seen" (MEV).

In chapter 34 Moses makes the plan to go up on Mount Sinai in the morning and talk with God. He was taking two more tablets for God to rewrite the commandments. The plan was for Moses to see the back of God's glory. God says in verse 3, "No one is to come with you" (NIV). So, Moses went up alone, and verse 5 says, "The LORD descended in the cloud and stood with him there, and proclaimed the name of the LORD."

Moses' response is found in verse 34:8; Moses hit the ground. He bowed to the ground and worshipped. Moses asked God for forgiveness for himself and the people. He was overwhelmed in the presence of the Lord. God made a covenant with Moses and the people and asked that they obey him. God wrote the covenant on the stone tablets, which are the Ten Commandments.

Moses came back down the mountain with the tablets, and the people were afraid because Moses' face glowed. Moses explained that the Lord had spoken to him on Mount Sinai. Moses' face was so bright he had to put a veil over it. Every time Moses went to speak with the Lord, he took the veil off. When he came out from speaking with the Lord, he would put the veil back over his face.

This is the presence of the Lord. When we spend time with the Father like this, we should come out changed.

Psalm 34:5 describes it this way: "They looked to Him [God] and became radiant, and their faces are not ashamed" (MEV).

His presence should change our countenance, our attitude, our words, our thinking. His presence is God's glory, and when His glory is revealed, we should become radiant and unashamed of who we are in Him.

The cool part about the veil is that Moses used this veil to separate himself from the rest. They were afraid of who he became when he spent time with the Lord. They wanted Moses to do it because the change caused fear in the hearts of the Israelites. Moses used the veil to cover up what the Lord gave him.

Moses was set apart from the rest because he chose to spend time with God. He didn't want to move unless God was coming too or told him to move. Moses longed for intimacy with the Lord, so much that he lived his life covered up when he was with his people. When he was with God, he walked uncovered, growing in and reflecting God's glory.

You can read about the Laws given to Moses and the

tabernacle starting in Exodus 20–34. It is hard to understand because it is so far removed from the way our Christian heritage is. But it helps you to get an understanding of the detail behind the sacrifices, the parts in the tabernacle, and God's design for sacrifice. When you read this, it makes you even more grateful for Jesus because there is no way we could do all this and match up. He was the atonement sacrifice. We don't have to do it all because of Him. Thank God for Jesus.

In order to grasp the importance of the veil, you need to see it in black and white. Earlier in Exodus the Israelites built a tabernacle to hold the presence of the Lord. The blueprint was given to them by God through Moses. Only the high priest, those from the tribe of Levi, were able to enter in the holy place called the Holy of Holies.

> BECAUSE OF THE ATONEMENT FOR ALL OUR SIN, THE VEIL WAS TORN. WE ARE NO LONGER SEPARATED FROM THE PRESENCE OF GOD.... THANK YOU, JESUS.

The high priest entered the most holy place one time a year for the day of atonement. There were special cleaning rituals and clothing in preparation to enter. They wore bells on their clothes in case they were struck dead by the glory. If the bell jingled because they were struck dead, those outside the holy place could pull the rope and drag the body out. Then the next priest would take the position and offer the sacrifices.

The tabernacle had a special place for the ark of the covenant, which was where the presence of the Lord rested. The mercy seat sat upon the top of the ark of the covenant. It consisted of two carved golden angels whose wings span wide and back and just about touched. The angels were upon the lid on the ark (box), which held the Ten Commandments.

The ark of the covenant had to be carried with special poles and not touched by human hands. The ark of the covenant was placed inside the Holy of Holies. Normal men could not enter or go anywhere near the most holy place. All this was behind a thick veil that separated the Holy Place from the Most Holy Place, the Holy of Holies.

The veil separated man from the presence of God. The people were afraid of God. They didn't know God like Moses did, nor did they try to. They had a fear of God that was unhealthy. They were afraid, not in awe. Moses' fear of God was a reverence for God's majesty and glory.

The veil separated. It separated man from God's presence. Only the chosen ones, the Levite priests, who were technically accredited "consecrated and holy," could enter in. But Jesus.

Jesus came and made the ultimate sacrifice on the cross for our sin. Because of the atonement for all our sin, the veil was torn. We are no longer separated from the presence of God. We do not have to be accredited as holy enough to spend time with God or sit in His presence. Thank you, Jesus.

In Matthew 27:51 we can read a quick rendition of the death of Jesus. It says that the moment Jesus released His Spirit and died, the veil, or curtain, of the temple was torn in two from the top to the bottom. The ground shook, the rocks split apart, and the graves were opened.

When Jesus tore the veil, the separation between God and man was no more. The veil was removed, and the presence of God was available to anyone who wanted to experience it. Glory to God. Sign me up, please!

The last spot I want to take you to is 2 Corinthians. Paul speaks of the new covenant that came from Jesus and the hope of glory we have in Him. It also talks about the power of the Holy Spirit that Jesus left as our Comforter when He returned to heaven to be with Father God.

Second Corinthians 3:7–8 says, "But if the ministry of death, written and engraved on stones, was glorious, so that the children of Israel could not look steadily at the face of Moses because of the glory of his countenance, which glory was passing away, how will the ministry of the Spirit not be more glorious?"

Verse 12 says, "Since we have such hope, we use great boldness of speech." We have the presence of God, the hope of Jesus, and the power of the Holy Spirit.

Then, in Hebrews 4:16, we are told to "come boldly to the throne of grace, that we may obtain mercy and find grace to help in time of need."

We can come boldly because we are no longer separated. We can come boldly because the payment has already been made by Jesus. We can come boldly and find the anointing of the Holy Spirit.

Look at 2 Corinthians 3:16–18: "Nevertheless when anyone turns to the Lord, the veil is removed. Now the Lord is the Spirit. And where the Spirit of the Lord is, there is liberty. But we all, seeing the glory of the Lord with unveiled faces, as in a mirror, are being transformed into the same image from glory to glory by the Spirit of the Lord."

Oh my goodness. Adam and Eve walked with God in the garden and had fellowship with Him. Moses saw just a glimpse of God's glory, and his countenance changed. The disciples walked with Jesus and saw miracles, people healed and set free from demons. We are even more blessed.

We have access to Father God anytime we want because the veil has been torn and we are no longer separated from His presence. We are no longer separated. All we have to do is believe and be saved and spend time with Jesus.

We have all the stories of Jesus from the Bible, and we get to have a personal relationship with Him as our Savior. On top of all that, we are given the third person on the trinity, the Holy Spirit. He is the One who gives us the authority to do the things Jesus did (John 14:12). Paul said if spending time with God changes your countenance, how much more glorious is the ministry of the Holy Spirit (2 Cor. 3:7–8)!

Imagine a world where Christians have daily encounters with the Holy Spirit and the presence of God. Imagine the countenances of Christians who walk in their calling and kingdom authority. The Holy Spirit wants to use you to change the world. Are you willing to come boldly and let Him?

21

THE HOLY SPIRIT

*D*on't close the book now.

Trust me. Trust God. Keep going.

This, this right here is the reason this book has taken so long. God wanted me to write this chapter and the next few. I argued and quit writing because of fear. He won.

Why did God want it in here so badly? Because God doesn't want you left behind. God doesn't want you to miss the rest of Him. God wants to give you all of Him. The Holy Spirit isn't scary; He's a gentleman. Just hang in there and keep going.

The Holy Spirit is a touchy subject even in church circles. Many people believe differently based on how they were raised, which denomination or religion they grew up in, and such. Some are just afraid of the unknown. Please bear with me and keep reading. If you disagree, OK. If you just don't understand, ask the Lord for clarity. I believe the Holy Spirit is just as important as God and Jesus. He is the third part of the Trinity. How can we fully know God and who we are in Him if we only accept two-thirds of Him?

When the Lord asked me to add this section on the Holy Spirit and what follows, I stopped writing, for several years. When people would ask me if I was done with my prayer book, I would claim writer's block. I was blocked; I was afraid. My fear held me back and kept me from writing. I was afraid because the subject of the Holy Spirit freaks people out. He shouldn't, but He does. I feel bad for Him because He is an integral piece to holding authority in prayer.

Did you know that the little nudge in your gut that tells you to leave that dirty movie or party is the Holy Spirit? Did you know that the little voice you hear telling you to stop talking, walk away, or not respond to that text is the Holy Spirit? Did you know that the feeling of peace you get when you are afraid and ask for God's help or even just saying, "Oh, Jesus," is the Holy Spirit? See, He's not scary. He's just a little buddy who is always by your side.

I always envision the red devil on one shoulder, talking to you, and the little angel on the other shoulder, talking. That little angel is the Holy Spirit. He is considered your conscience, in a way. If you have asked Jesus into your heart and made Him your Savior, you were given access to God the Father, God the Son, and God the Holy Spirit in that moment. You were given the full Trinity, full access.

Here's a glimpse of how that works. You sin, and the Holy Spirit nudges you to stop and repent. Jesus has already paid for it, so your sin is forgiven. Jesus paid your debt and defends you to the Father; God wipes your slate clean. The Bible says that God's forgiveness is "as far as the east is from the west, so far has He removed our transgressions [sins] from us" (Ps. 103:12).

All three parts of the Trinity were present at creation. There are two passages that prove this. The first is Genesis 1:1–2: "In the beginning God created the heavens and the earth. The earth was formless and void, darkness was over the surface of the deep, and the Spirit of God was moving over the surface of the water" (MEV). This is the very first book, chapter, and verse of the Bible. It talks about God and the Spirit. Then, in the next verse, God speaks and begins to form the earth. This represents Jesus.

How does this represent Jesus? Let's jump to the New Testament Book of John. In John 1:1, which shows us Jesus in the Old Testament, John says, "In the beginning was the

Word, and the Word was with God, and the Word was God." The Word here, spelled with a capital W, is Jesus. John 1:14 says, "The Word became flesh and dwelt among us, and we saw His glory, the glory as the only Son of the Father, full of grace and truth" (MEV). Jesus is the Word of God spoken out at creation. Jesus is also the Word that became flesh, or man, and dwelt on earth.

John then goes on to say in verses 2:5, "He was in the beginning with God. All things were made through him, and without Him nothing was made that was made. In Him was life, and the life was the light of men." Jesus is then explained as the Light that John the Baptist is sent ahead of time to prepare the way for.

Jesus is called the true Light, the Word, and the Lamb of God all before the chapter ends. All the label/naming words are in capital form for expression. These verses explain who each person of the Trinity is, their part at creation, and the proof they all existed at creation.

We've talked about those who were alive to walk and talk with God and the disciples who lived during Jesus' life on earth. We are the ones the Bible calls "those who have not seen and yet have believed" (John 20:29) but get the benefit of the Holy Spirit.

What is the benefit of the Holy Spirit?

We talked in the previous chapter about how we have the authority from the Holy Spirit to do the things Jesus did. Let's start there.

Found in John 14:12 (red letters mean Jesus is speaking), Jesus says, "Most assuredly, I say to you, he who believes in Me, the works that I do he will do also; and greater works than these he will do, because I go to My Father."

Then, in John 16:5–7, Jesus says, "But now I go away to Him who sent Me, and none of you asks Me, 'Where are You going?' But because I have said these things to you, sorrow has filled your heart. Nevertheless I tell you the truth. It is to your advantage that I go away; for if I do not go away, the Helper will not come to you; but if I depart, I will send Him to you."

John 16:13–15 says, "When the Spirit of truth comes, He will guide you into all truth. For He will not speak on His own authority. But He will speak whatever He hears, and He will tell you things that are to come. He will glorify Me, for He will receive from Me and will declare it to you. All that the Father has is Mine. Therefore I said that He will take what is Mine and will declare it to you" (MEV).

So basically, if Jesus didn't go back to heaven to hang with Father God until we get there, the Holy Spirit couldn't come. But when Jesus left, He sent the Holy Spirit so we could get info from heaven.

In these verses John describes the Holy Spirit in these ways:

- The Spirit of truth
- Guides you into all truth
- Won't speak on own authority
- Speaks whatever He hears
- Tells you things to come
- Glorifies God
- Receives from God
- Declares it to you

Not only that, but He will also help us do what Jesus did here on earth. What? This is a part of God I want. I don't know about you, but who wants a personal truth-speaking counselor with direct contact to God in heaven giving information to me about my life? Is your hand lifted? Mine is. Where do I sign?

This is who the Holy Spirit is. He's not scary. He's your helper, guide, and comforter.

Now, before we get to the part of Jesus sending us the Holy Spirit when He ascended to heaven, I want to show you the importance of the Holy Spirit—also, Jesus giving and receiving the Holy Spirit. From the Book of John, flip backward one book. Let's look at who John the Baptist is and how this all began.

I just *love* the story of John the Baptist. I'm going to break it down so you can see how awesome it is. Turn to Luke 1.

THIS IS WHO THE HOLY SPIRIT IS. HE'S NOT SCARY. HE'S YOUR HELPER, GUIDE, AND COMFORTER.

The angel Gabriel appeared to Zechariah, a priest in the temple, and his wife, Elizabeth. Now Elizabeth was old and barren; she and Zechariah were both upright in the sight of God. The angel told them they would have a son who is to be set apart as a chosen one of God. Here are the requests/requirements:

1. Never to drink any alcohol
2. Filled with the Holy Spirit from birth
3. He will bring people back to the Lord
4. Have the power of Elijah and walk in the spirit
5. Turn hearts of man from disobedient back to righteousness
6. Prepare the way of the Lord

Zechariah questions the angel Gabriel and is struck dumb, or mute. His mouth got him into trouble, so the angel shut his mouth. He told Zechariah he wouldn't be able to speak until the words he had told them came to pass.

Meanwhile in Nazareth, Gabriel visited the virgin Mary and told her she would become pregnant by the Holy Spirit. Gabriel told Mary about Elizabeth being pregnant and told her, "Nothing is impossible with God."

So, Mary went to visit her relative Elizabeth. When she got there, the unborn baby in Elizabeth's womb leapt for joy. In that moment, Elizabeth was filled with the Holy Spirit.

Power entered the room in the form of an unborn child in Mary's womb, and the power of the Holy Spirit came upon the other woman in the room. So cool! Elizabeth spoke a word of blessing over her relative Mary. Mary followed the blessing by singing a song of worship. These women use their mouths to honor and believe the power of the Lord.

"Death and life are in the power of the tongue" (Prov. 18:21). Mary and Elizabeth used this incredible moment to worship God. Back then, it was BC, before Christ. There wasn't a salvation that came through Jesus. They didn't get the Holy Spirit at salvation. They only could trust and follow God.

Mary was a teenager; Elizabeth was her elder relative. The women were not allowed to read the Torah. The only way they knew about God was if their fathers or husbands shared with them and they chose to believe. Mary was visited by an angel and impregnated by the Holy Spirit. That would make you believe. Elizabeth had a cousin visit and got filled with the Holy Spirit. This story is legendary.

Later, when Elizabeth had her baby, the townspeople expected her to name him after his father, but she said, "No, his name is John." They asked his father, Zechariah, and he agreed and wrote on a tablet, "His name is John." The moment he obeyed, his tongue was loosed and he began to praise the Lord. He was immediately filled with the Holy Spirit and began to prophesy. Obedience led to a release of the power of the Holy Spirit.

Zechariah couldn't speak until he obeyed. Then his tongue was loosed and he prophesied. Guys, this is all part of the Bible showing us that the power and gifts of the Holy Spirit are real. Keep reading.

John the Baptist was born full of the Holy Spirit. His parents both were filled with the Holy Spirit as a result of his birth. They used their mouths to glorify God. The baby Jesus, who wasn't even born yet, who was sent to be the Savior of the world, started it by coming with power.

Jesus in the womb of Mary was *so* full of the power of the Holy Spirit, he transferred it to Elizabeth from the womb. John, inside the womb, also received the Holy Spirit. Remember, it was promised he would be full of spirit at birth. All from in utero, Jesus coming into the room with His mom brought some serious power. We have seen Jesus bringing the Holy Spirit to Mary, Elizabeth, Zechariah, and John all before Jesus was born. Apparently, the Holy Spirit is pretty important.

Spirit-filled baby John grew up and was sent to prepare the way for Jesus. Back in John 1, the Bible talks about John growing up and people thinking he was the Christ because he baptized people. When asked why he baptized, he replied, "I baptize with water, but there stands One among you whom you do not know. It is He who, coming after me, is preferred before me, whose sandal strap I am not worthy to loose" (John 1:26–27).

Now we know about the Trinity: God the Father; God the Son, Jesus; and God the Holy Spirit. We know that they were all present at creation. We know they are all equally important. We know that the Holy Spirit was around and moving in the beginning but also throughout Scripture.

The Holy Spirit prepared the way for Jesus. Jesus prepared the way for the Holy Spirit. Let's jump into what both of those look like next.

22

THE BAPTISM OF JESUS AND THE COMING OF THE HOLY SPIRIT

W LEARNED ABOUT the relationship between John and Jesus and their mothers from our previous chapter. John may not have known that Jesus was the Messiah, but he did know that a Messiah was coming, because his parents taught him that. We don't hear about them playing as kids. But we do know about before they reunited.

The coming of the Messiah had been prophesied in Isaiah 40:3: "A voice of one calling: 'In the wilderness prepare the way for the LORD; make straight in the desert a highway for our God'" (NIV).

When John became a minister, he did everything he could to spread the word about the coming Messiah. He would tell the people to repent, for the kingdom of heaven is near. They would confess their sins, and then he would baptize them in the Jordan River. He would baptize with water to represent the repentance in the washing away of sin that comes after salvation.

In Matthew 3:11, John says, "I baptize you with water for repentance. But after me comes one who is more powerful than I, whose sandals I am not worthy to carry. He will baptize you with the Holy Spirit and fire" (NIV).

Because of John's ministry he became known as John the Baptist, because he was the baptizer. The people of the Judean countryside and Jerusalem came to the Jordan River to meet with John and hear of this Messiah and be baptized.

In Matthew's account in chapter 3 verse 11, John tells them

that Jesus will baptize them with the Holy Spirit and with fire. "His winnowing fork is in his hand, and he will clear his threshing floor, gathering his wheat into the barn and burning up the chaff with unquenchable fire" (v. 12, NIV).

In Mark's account in chapter 1 he explains about John. It says, "John will baptize with water, but the coming one will baptize you with the Holy Spirit."

In Luke's account in chapter 3, starting in verse 16, John answered the people waiting with these words: "I baptize you with water. But one who is more powerful than I will come, the straps of whose sandals I am not worthy to untie. He will baptize you with the Holy Spirit and fire. His winnowing fork is in his hand to clear his threshing floor and to gather the wheat into his barn, but he will burn up the chaff with unquenchable fire."

In Matthew's account at the end of chapter 3, he speaks of heaven opening and seeing the spirit of God descending like a dove and alighting on Jesus and hearing the voice from heaven: "This is my Son, whom I love; with him I am well pleased" (Matt. 3:17, NIV).

In chapter 4, Jesus was led by the spirit into the desert to be tempted by the devil, and He fasted forty days and forty nights.

In Mark's account in chapter 1, Mark saw Jesus come up out of the water, and he saw heaven being torn open and the spirit descending on him like a dove. Then he heard an audible voice that came from heaven saying, "You are my son, whom I love; with you I am well pleased."

In Luke's account, chapter 3, verse 21, when all the people were baptized, Jesus was baptized too. And as He was praying, heaven was opened and the Holy Spirit descended on him in bodily form like a dove. And a voice came from heaven saying, "You are my Son, whom I love; with you I am well pleased."

All the gospel accounts of what happened when John baptized Jesus say the same thing because these men were there. Their identical descriptions help us determine the accuracy and authenticity of this event.

Jesus was about thirty years old when He began His ministry. Luke 4:1 says, "Jesus, being filled with the Holy Spirit, returned from the Jordan and was led by the Spirit into the wilderness, being tempted for forty days by the devil."

IF JESUS NEEDED THE HOLY SPIRIT, WE DO TOO.

John's account is found in chapter 1 starting in verse 19, where the people are asking John who he is. John's reply to them comes in verse 23, where John replied in the words of Isaiah the prophet: "I am the voice of one calling in the wilderness, 'Make straight the way for the Lord'" (NIV).

John is the road grader preparing the way of the Lord. And the Pharisees questioned him and asked him why he was baptizing if he was not the Christ. He responded in John 1:26–27, "I baptize with water…but among you stands one you do not know. He is the one who comes after me, the straps of whose sandals I am not worthy to untie" (NIV). All this took place in Bethany on the other side of the Jordan River where John was baptizing.

> The next day John saw Jesus coming toward him and said, "Look, the Lamb of God, who takes away the sin of the world! This is the one I meant when I said, 'A man who comes after me has surpassed me because he was before me.' I myself did not know him, but the reason I came baptizing with water was that he might be revealed to Israel."
> —JOHN 1:29–31, NIV

Then John gave this testimony in John 1:32–33:

I saw the Spirit descending from heaven like a dove, and He remained upon Him. I did not know Him, but He who sent me to baptize with water said to me, 'Upon whom you see the Spirit descending, and remaining on Him, this is He who baptizes with the Holy Spirit.' And I have seen and testified that this is the Son of God.

After Jesus was baptized, He traveled into the desert and was tempted by the devil for forty days and forty nights, where he fasted and prayed. He needed the Holy Spirit to face this. His first miracle at the wedding of Cana followed, and then all throughout his life the miracles were part of His life story. All this is to say that if Jesus needed the Holy Spirit, we do too.

He needed the power and authority of the Holy Spirit to do as the Father told Him to do. The power and authority are something we can all use. There is so much more to the Holy Spirit. We will discuss the authority, the gifts, and prayer next.

23

GIFTS OF THE HOLY SPIRIT

*T*HE FRUITS AND gifts of the Holy Spirit are biblical but totally different. Each of them have to do with how your life represents Jesus.

The fruit of the spirit is found in Galatians 5:22–23: "The fruit of the Spirit is love, joy, peace, patience, gentleness, goodness, faith, meekness, and self-control; against such there is no law" (MEV).

Paul speaks to the church of Galatia about how to live the Christian life. If you want to follow Jesus, you want to walk in the Spirit and not fulfill the lust of the flesh. He explains the sins of the flesh that tend to try and rule mankind in the previous verses. Then, he suggests the attributes that a person who follows Christ and wants to live by the Spirit would take on.

Most Christians know about the fruits of the Spirit, but not all know about the gifts of the Spirit, otherwise known as spiritual gifts. These are found in 1 Corinthians 12:7–11. However, I would like to start at the beginning of chapter 12 because it helps us understand the why of the gifts.

> Now about the gifts of the Spirit, brothers and sisters, I do not want you to be uninformed. You know that when you were pagans, somehow or other you were influenced and led astray to mute idols. Therefore I want you to know that no one who is speaking by the Spirit of God says, "Jesus be cursed," and no one can say, "Jesus is Lord," except by the Holy Spirit. There are different kinds of gifts, but the same Spirit distributes them. There are different

kinds of service, but the same Lord. There are different kinds of working, but in all of them and in everyone it is the same God at work. Now to each one the manifestation of the Spirit is given for the common good. To one there is given through the Spirit a message of wisdom, to another a message of knowledge by means of the same Spirit, to another faith by the same Spirit, to another gifts of healing by that one Spirit, to another miraculous powers, to another prophecy, to another distinguishing between spirits, to another speaking in different kinds of tongues, and to still another the interpretation of tongues. All these are the work of one and the same Spirit, and he distributes them to each one, just as he determines.

—1 CORINTHIANS 12:1–11

If you have never seen these, you may be totally confused. Remember, you get the Holy Spirit when you accept Jesus as your Savior. You don't have to do anything. I heard a pastor say once that the Holy Spirit we receive when we come into the family of God is called the indwelling. The Spirit of God indwells in us at salvation. We join the family of God and live with His presence all the time. We dwell together. The Holy Spirit dwells with us.

The spiritual gifts of the Holy Spirit are what verse 7 calls a manifestation, basically, the proof you are walking and living with the Holy Spirit controlling you. It's allowing God to operate in you.

Some people call it "baptism in the Holy Spirit" because it is like a fresh anointing of the Spirit falling on you when you ask God for more and to give you the gifts He desires for you to walk in. The manifestation of it is when you are able to do one. You may not get them all. You may get a couple, and then later another. You may just get one, and God will grow you in your use of that one.

Let me explain what they are before we go deeper.

The Greek word for a spiritual gift is *charismata*. It is an extraordinary power given as a free gift by God through the Holy Spirit. They are a blessing to people who want to go deeper with the Lord and grow in their love for Him.

1. Word of wisdom
2. Word of knowledge
3. Faith
4. Healing
5. Working of miracles
6. Prophecy
7. Discerning of spirits
8. Various kinds of tongues
9. Interpretation of tongues

I picture a shelf full of nine beautifully wrapped gifts. Each present is labeled "To: you" and "From: God." You ask God to come into your life and take control. You give Him your heart and make Him your Savior. You choose to change your lifestyle to represent one that looks like what His Word says. You stay away from the worldly and fleshly desires. Basically, you're choosing to walk in the Spirit rather than in the flesh, as Galatians 5 talks about. Reading the Bible, praying, and developing your relationship with Christ will cause you to want more of Him in your life.

When you reach this place of wanting more of God, you will begin to desire all He has to offer. Ask the Father for a gift. Pray and seek Him until you see one manifest.

Gifts are where you see the power and gain the authority. These gifts are supernatural, which means they are beyond your doing. They are God at work within you. Supernatural gifts are signs and wonders. They are not done in your own power but through the power of the Holy Spirit living in you.

Jesus performed these signs and wonders. In Acts 2:22 Peter tells the men of Israel, "Jesus of Nazareth was a man attested to you by God with powerful works and wonders and signs, which God did through Him in your midst" (MEV).

The Gospels of Matthew, Mark, Luke, and John all tell of the life of Jesus and His miracles, signs, and wonders. Whether Jesus multiplied a child's lunch to feed thousands, healed the lame, blind, deaf, and mute, or delivered people from demonic sprits, He was performing signs and wonders.

Matthew 24:14 says, "And this gospel of the kingdom will be preached in all the world as a witness to all the nations, and then the end will come." When the gospel is preached, followed by a sign or wonder, the authenticity of the gospel is the proof, or witness, of the power of the gospel.

"By Him [Jesus] you are enriched in everything, in all speech and in all knowledge, even as the testimony of Christ was confirmed in you, so that you are not lacking in any gift while waiting for the revelation of our Lord Jesus Christ" (1 Cor. 1:5–7, MEV).

God has all these gifts at your disposal if you want them. When you choose to walk in the authority of the gifts, you are "not lacking in any gift," as Paul writes. God wants us to desire them and not be afraid of them.

When people start talking about the gifts, some get antsy and scared. The Holy Spirit is a gentleman. He isn't going to give you a gift you don't want or force you to do something to embarrass yourself. That is not how He works. He also does not give the gifts for personal gain but to help the church and grow your faith. Remember, the gifts bear witness to the power of the gospel.

Any believer can walk in these gifts, but your God wants

you to "eagerly desire" them (1 Cor. 14:1, NIV). You may already have them lying dormant, and if you ask God for more of Him, He may reveal them. Let's look at 1 Corinthians 14:1: "Follow the way of love and eagerly desire gifts of the Spirit, especially prophecy" (NIV).

God wants us to grow in the gifts of the Holy Spirit.

> For anyone who speaks in a tongue does not speak to people but to God. Indeed, no one understands them; they utter mysteries by the Spirit. But the one who prophesies speaks to people for their strengthening, encouraging and comfort. Anyone who speaks in a tongue edifies themselves, but the one who prophesies edifies the church. I would like every one of you to speak in tongues, but I would rather have you prophesy. The one who prophesies is greater than the one who speaks in tongues, unless someone interprets, so that the church may be edified.
>
> —vv. 2–5, NIV

The power comes when we dig deeper into our relationship with God and desire more. We can live our entire Christian lives getting by and still making a difference but not grasping the power we have from the Holy Spirit. It's a gift on a shelf we decide to leave unopened because we don't understand it or are scared. As a gentleman, the Holy Spirit won't ask you to do something weird. He just wants to empower you.

One of the best books I have read that helps you understand the gifts well is by Havilah Cunnington and named *Discovering and Activating My Spiritual Gifts*; it is available on Amazon. Cunnington does an excellent job explaining the reason for and the use of the gifts. If you have any interest in learning more and activating your gifts with a little help, grab this book. It is a fifteen-day journey, and you will feel knowledgeable and less afraid when you are finished.

Another source I use is the Spritual Warfare Bible as my study Bible. I use this Bible as my study Bible because I like the additional warfare commentary inside. Most Bibles have additional nuggets of information from commentary or books written by wise and trustworthy authors. One of the pages explains the gifts and gives their definition. I will list them again but with their definitions as provided in my Bible.

1. Word of Wisdom is the ability to impart wisdom from God's Word.

2. Word of Knowledge is special knowledge that empowers us for warfare and ministry.

3. Faith is special faith to trust God for the impossible.

4. Healing is the power to heal the sick.

5. Working of miracles is power to perform miracles that point to Jesus.

6. Prophecy is prophetically speaking God's Word to encourage, build up, exhort, and caution.

7. Discerning of spirits is understanding and identifying the demonic manifestations at work.

8. Various kinds of tongues is an unknown language in which the Holy Spirit prays through us.

9. Interpretation of tongues is the gift of interpreting unknown tongues.

This list is taken from the Holy Spirit Encounter Bible.

These gifts are life-giving filling, or manifestations, of the Holy Spirit. As believers we can walk in empowerment and authority because of Jesus. The same power of signs and wonders Jesus' walked in is poured out, or "upon," us to walk in abundant life, not lacking.

Jesus said in John 14:12–14 (NIV), "Very truly I tell you, whoever believes in me will do the works I have been doing, and they will do even greater things than these, because I am going to the Father. And I will do whatever you ask in my name, so that the Father may be glorified in the Son. You may ask me for anything in my name, and I will do it."

When Jesus went to the Father and ascended to heaven, He sent the Holy Spirit so we could do all He did and more, not for our own glorification but for His glory. To bear witness of His glory and power and represent Him well. To build our faith, our communities' faith, and empower others to desire more of the things of God. Oh, how He loves us.

Now that you know what these are, you can pray about whether you want them to be part of your life. These gifts and the Holy Spirit are such a part of who I am. These sections are the chapters I knew I needed to write but held off until the Lord made it clear and I had no other option but to obey. He wanted them in here so that you would be aware.

Not all churches and denominations teach this, but I was blessed to be raised in a church community that walked in the Spirit. Also, my grandfather was a Spirit-filled pastor. When I was a little girl, we would visit his home and his church. I witnessed the power of the Holy Spirit at a young age.

> WHEN JESUS WENT TO THE FATHER AND ASCENDED TO HEAVEN, HE SENT THE HOLY SPIRIT SO WE COULD DO ALL HE DID AND MORE.

I remember being in his game room as a preteen and a man coming over to be prayed for and watching them gather around him and pray for his leg to grow. It did. This is the gift of healing.

A close friend told me about when she began to desire the gifts and her hands got hot. She heard in her spirit to ask to pray for the lady in front of her. She tapped the lady and asked to pray for her and the lady needed prayer for her back. My friend prayed for the lady, and the heat stayed in her hands and then left. This is a manifestation of the gift of healing.

I remember the first time I heard someone speak in tongues. I was around nine or ten and was sitting in Sunday "big church" with my parents. A man from the congregation spoke loudly, and my sister and I looked at each other and giggled. We had no idea what was going on. My mom looked at us, shook her head no, and said, "No, ma'am. Shh, I will explain later." We shrugged, and the next thing we knew, another man said something out loud in English from the other side of the room. My mom later explained to us that these were gifts of the Holy Spirit and we should never laugh but desire the gifts. This story speaks of two gifts. The man who spoke in a weird language was using his prayer language, which is the gift of unknown tongues. The man who spoke in English was using his gift of interpretation of tongues.

A friend's daughter wanted a puppy and told her mother she had been praying for a puppy. The mother kept telling her daughter, "Not right now." The little girl would reply, "I'm asking God for one." The little girl continued to pray, and one day they went to an event in which there was a drawing for different items. The little girl entered her name, and she told her mother, "God's going to give me a puppy." The mother didn't want to discourage her daughters' faith, but she also didn't want her to get her hopes up and get disappointed. Sure enough, the little girls' name was called, and they walked out with a white lab puppy. She named the puppy Maximum Faith and called him Max. This little girl had the gift of faith, she believed God, and when she asked, He delivered. This didn't grow the faith of only the little girl but also her mother.

Another friend of mine wanted her prayer language and started asking the Lord for it. She would sit and wait. She decided to just worship the Lord and listen and wait. She was desiring the gift, and the Lord deposited a spiritual language in her mouth. She only had a couple of words to begin with, but the more she used it, the more words she received. Now it is a huge part of her life and ministry. This is the gift of tongues.

A few years ago a friend and I decided to do a prayer walk at our public school. We ended up both being able to go on a Saturday. We started by walking around the perimeter of the school and placing a rock on each corner we came to and praying. They had Saturday school going, so we were able to get in. Isn't that just like Jesus? The longer we prayed, the more the Holy Spirit began to manifest in and through us. I would walk up to a door of the school and feel pressure and knew it was like a demonic oppression. So I would pray in the Spirit, using my prayer language, and motion for her to come over. When she walked over, she would begin praying in English and breaking the demonic strongholds she was feeling in that area. It was very powerful. The gifts manifested here are various kinds of tongues and discerning of spirits.

This is explained in Romans 12:4–5: "For just as we have many parts in one body, and not all parts have the same function, so we, being many, are one body in Christ, and all are parts of one another" (MEV).

I have been blessed to have a lifetime of seeing the Holy Spirit manifest in myself and others. I have also seen the power and authority that comes with allowing the Holy Spirit to be at work in my life. I hope my explanations and personal experiences have helped you understand and desire the gifts for yourself. Choosing to surrender to the Holy Spirit is a choice you will never regret.

24

FRUIT OF THE SPIRIT AND THE WORKING OF THE HOLY SPIRIT

*T*HE GIFTS OF the Holy Spirit are different from the fruit of the Holy Spirit.

The Holy Spirit empowers us to reject sin and choose holiness. He empowers us to walk toward the ways of the Lord and away from the ways of the world. He gives us fruit that will bless our lives and others. The fruit of the Holy Spirit is found in Galatians 5:22–23. They are love, joy, peace, patience, kindness, goodness, faithfulness, gentleness, and self-control.

The more you draw near to the Lord, the more you will begin to carry these fruits. The world says we are not to judge, and maybe not. The Bible says, "The tree will be known by its fruit" (Matt. 12:33).

> A good man out of the good treasure of his heart brings forth good things. And an evil man out of the evil treasure brings forth evil things.
>
> —MATTHEW 12:35, MEV

You may not be able to judge a book by its cover, but you can judge a tree by its fruit. If you are a tree, what kind of fruit are you bearing? If your family and friends come and sit in the shade of your tree and eat of the fruit, what kind of fruit are they eating? Is it bitter and moldy? Or are you dishing out love, joy, peace, patience, kindness, goodness, faithfulness, gentleness and self-control?

We want to represent Jesus with the fruit of our lives. In John 15:12 Jesus said, "This is My commandment, that you love one another as I have loved you." Then he concludes in John 15:16, "I appointed you to go and bear fruit, fruit that will last" (NRSVUE).

Our lives tell a story of how we live and if we represent God. The more we desire the things of God and the fruit and gifts of the Holy Spirit, the more we truly become Christlike. We stop desiring the things of the world and start desiring only the things of the Lord. Our lives and fruit will represent that. So will our ability to battle the enemy. Satan loses power when we walk in the Spirit.

The Holy Spirit empowers us to fight the enemy, the devil, and his army. He enables us by the armor of God to fight the battles of spiritual warfare that we face every single day.

The Holy Spirit is where the power is. Jesus brought it with Him into Mary, passed it to Elizabeth and John the Baptist, then to his father Zechariah. The Holy Spirit landed on Jesus the moment of His baptism in the form of a dove and lightning in Matthew 3:16.

The Holy Spirit fell in flaming tongues from a violent wind from heaven on the believers in the Upper Room on the day of Pentecost. The Holy Spirit is available to you if you are a believer. He comes at salvation, and His power comes by belief.

I know in my own life I couldn't have made it without the Holy Spirit. When I say the Holy Spirit comes in power, I mean authority. He grants you authority to proclaim God's promises for yourself and your family. He gives you boldness to declare things you cannot see in the physical but can believe for spiritually.

Acts is a book in the Bible that many choose to overlook and not preach on. Since I held back for so long and wouldn't write about it, now you get to hear it all. Let's talk about baptism and the Holy Spirit. If your Bible isn't out, grab it and go to Acts in the New Testament.

Acts is the book in the Bible where the Holy Spirit acts. Here Jesus has died and risen again. He is about to ascend to heaven and told the apostles and all His followers to wait on the Holy Spirit. He had promised them He would send a helper, or Counselor, the Holy Spirit.

John 16:7 (AMP) says, "But I tell you the truth, it is to your advantage that I go away; for if I do not go away, the Helper (Comforter, Advocate, Intercessor—Counselor, Strengthener, Standby) will not come to you; but if I go, I will send Him (the Holy Spirit) to you [to be in close fellowship with you]."

The Amplified Bible explains this so well. Look at all Jesus calls the Holy Spirit. I'll take one of those, please, and make it a large. Back to Acts 1.

Jesus is standing there with His apostles after His resurrection, and He was with them forty days. He tells them two major things, then ascends to heaven.

1. John baptized with water, but you shall be baptized with the Holy Spirit not many days from now (Acts 1:5).

2. But you shall receive power when the Holy Spirit comes upon you (Acts 1:8).

OK, if the Holy Spirit, outside of just being one of the Trinity, is new to you, this is a wowza moment. Take a breath, and I will explain.

Let's start with number 1.

John the Baptist, who we talked about was a friend of Jesus, was "filled" with the Holy Spirit in his mother's womb just because Mary, Jesus' mother, walked into the room. He was the guy who baptized everyone in water and told of "another" coming. He was talking about Jesus. Now to backtrack just a bit, John baptized Jesus. When this happened, the dove descended on Jesus and God spoke from heaven. Are you remembering the story now?

John baptized with water. Jesus was baptized with water, then the Holy Spirit (in the form of a dove) came down upon Jesus. Jesus was baptized with water and the Holy Spirit. This was the Spirit (Holy Spirit) of God descending upon Jesus.

As I mentioned, you get the Holy Spirit at salvation, just as you get Jesus and God. They go together. But the baptism in the Holy Spirit is just the Holy Spirit, an empowerment that equips you for spiritual warfare and walking in boldness. Before we get too far, let's look at what happened on the day of Pentecost to explain how the Holy Spirit at salvation is different from baptism in the Holy Spirit.

Acts 2: I will start in verse 1 and quote it, then just shorten the story to explain. But you can read the entire story in Acts 2.

> When the day of Pentecost came, they were all together in one place. Suddenly a sound like the blowing of a violent wind came from heaven and filled the whole house where they were sitting. They saw what seemed to be tongues of fire that separated and came to rest on each of them. All of them were filled with the Holy Spirit and began to speak in other tongues as the Spirit enabled them.
>
> —ACTS 2:1–4, NIV

The apostles were celebrating the Feast of Weeks at the time, and Jesus was about to ascend to heaven. The day of Pentecost is considered the birthday of the church and the day the Holy Spirit entered into the room and filled the apostles.

Let's look at what this says happened:

1. A blowing violent wind came from heaven and filled the whole house.
2. Tongues of fire came, separated, and came to rest on each of them.
3. They were filled with the Holy Spirit.
4. They began to speak in tongues.

We discussed how one of the gifts of the Holy Spirit is various tongues. Some people call this a prayer language. It is a language between your spirit and the Holy Spirit. It is also called speaking in tongues. It is a manifestation of the power of the Holy Spirit. Not everyone gets this at baptism in the Holy Spirt, but it is one of the gifts.

Matthew 3:11 told us that John would baptize in water, and another (Jesus) would come and would baptize in the Holy Spirit and fire. This explains the tongues of fire that came. Can you imagine seeing flames that looked like a tongue coming and resting on you, and all of a sudden you start talking in a language you do not know or understand. Crazy stuff, right?

This is one of the gifts of the Holy Spirit that scares people because it is hard to understand it. But the Bible explains it so well by explaining before Jesus comes about water baptism and then Holy Spirit baptism. Matthew even mentions the Holy Spirit and fire being together. Remember in Exodus when the presence of God followed the Israelites in a pillar of cloud by day and a pillar of fire by night. The fire is the presence of God in the form of the Holy Spirit. Don't let the fire or the tongue scare you. It is part of the glory and presence of God.

Continuing in Acts 2:3–12, all the people heard them speaking and were blown away because they all heard them speaking in their own native language. God works in ways we cannot understand. Imagine hearing a message about

Jesus and not understanding the language and never knowing what they said. This day, the people came into town and heard about Jesus in their native language. Even those standing near a person from another country heard it and understood it as well. God wants His Word shared and will do what He needs to do to make it happen.

The Holy Spirit empowers and enables you to be bold and do something you wouldn't normally do. Not in a scary, out-of-control way, but a filling of more of God than ever before. Imagine a current of God just giving you a boost—that is what the baptism in the Holy Spirit is like. I'm just telling you about it how I know it. I can only speak for my own personal experiences to help you understand.

The people thought they were drunk on new wine. I have heard people currently say that speaking in tongues is of the devil or people are crazy who do it. The reason people are afraid of it and call it crazy is because they don't understand it. When people don't understand something or have never experienced it, they automatically judge it negatively. Don't allow yourself to go there. It is real. It is biblical. The Holy Spirit is part of the Trinity.

Next comes Peter's speech. We didn't talk about this, but Peter is the disciple who denied Jesus three times when asked if he was with Jesus as the Savior was getting beaten in the town square before His crucifixion. Jesus told Peter he would deny Him, and then he did. The same Peter who was afraid to admit he was a friend of Jesus became the first pastor of the first church in the history of churches. Peter's speech, his first sermon to the crowd, is found in Acts 2:14–39. This is the power of the Holy Spirit.

> Then Peter stood up with the Eleven, raised his voice and addressed the crowd: "Fellow Jews and all of you who live in Jerusalem, let me explain this to you; listen

carefully to what I say. These people are not drunk, as you suppose. It's only nine in the morning! No, this is what was spoken by the prophet Joel: 'In the last days, God says, I will pour out my Spirit on all people. Your sons and daughters will *prophesy*, your young men will see *visions*, your old men will dream *dreams*. Even on my servants, both men and women, *I will pour out my Spirit* in those days, and they will *prophesy*. I will show *wonders* in the heavens above and *signs* on the earth below, blood and fire and billows of smoke. The sun will be turned to darkness and the moon to blood before the coming of the great and glorious day of the Lord. And everyone who calls on the name of the Lord will be saved.'

Verses 22–28:

"Fellow Israelites, listen to this: Jesus of Nazareth was a man accredited by God to you by miracles, wonders and signs, which God did among you through him, as you yourselves know. This man was handed over to you by God's deliberate plan and foreknowledge; and you, with the help of wicked men, put him to death by nailing him to the cross. But God raised him from the dead, freeing him from the agony of death, because it was impossible for death to keep its hold on him. David said about him: 'I saw the Lord always before me. Because he is at my right hand, I will not be shaken. Therefore my heart is glad and my tongue rejoices; my body also will rest in hope, because you will not abandon me to the realm of the dead, you will not let your holy one see decay. You have made known to me the paths of life; you will fill me with joy in your presence.'

Verses 29–37:

"Fellow Israelites, I can tell you confidently that the patriarch David died and was buried, and his tomb is here to this day. But he was a prophet and knew that God had promised him on oath that he would place one of his descendants on his throne. Seeing what was to come, he spoke of the resurrection of the Messiah, that he was not abandoned to the realm of the dead, nor did his body see decay. God has raised this Jesus to life, and we are all witnesses of it. Exalted to the right hand of God, he has received from the Father the promised Holy Spirit and has poured out what you now see and hear. For David did not ascend to heaven, and yet he said, 'The Lord said to my Lord: "Sit at my right hand until I make your enemies a footstool for your feet."' Therefore let all Israel be assured of this: God has made this Jesus, whom you crucified, both Lord and Messiah." When the people heard this, they were cut to the heart and said to Peter and the other apostles, "Brothers, what shall we do?"

Verses 38–39:

Peter replied, *"Repent and be baptized, every one of you, in the name of Jesus Christ for the forgiveness of your sins. And you will receive the gift of the Holy Spirit.* The promise is for you and your children and for all who are far off—for all whom the Lord our God will call."
—Acts 2:14–39, niv, emphasis added

Peter got up after being baptized in the Holy Spirit and preached to the hundreds gathered. He told them about Jesus and how he had fulfilled the prophecies about His coming and how He would come again. He also told them about the *signs and wonders that would follow in us.* (I have italicized these words so you can spot them quickly.) Peter explained they should repent and be baptized and receive the gift of the Holy

Spirit. On top of all of that, they all heard him speak in their own personal language.

Is anyone else sitting here, mind blown?

God still moves like this today. Revivals are breaking out on college campuses. The Holy Spirit is still living and active. You can receive the gifts and power of the Holy Spirit; you just have to ask. God wants to impart all of Him upon you. Did you see the last part in verse 39? "The promise is for you and your children." Glory to God.

YOU HAVE THE POWER TO DEFEAT THE ENEMY AND STAND MORE FIRM IN THE TRUTH OF GOD'S WORD. THE POWER TO RESIST TEMPTATION AND SIN. THE POWER TO STAND UP FOR GOD AND NOT BE CONFORMED TO THE PATTERNS OF THIS WORLD.

The miracles that happened in the Bible did not stop when John put the last period in Revelation 22. God is still the Creator of the universe and the only true living God. Jesus is still in heaven with Father God interceding for you. He died for you and desires for you to be saved and serve Him in full surrender of your life. The Holy Spirit is not a ghost to be afraid of. The power to defeat sin and hell are in Him and available to you.

The power and majesty of the God of the Bible did not cease. He is still moving. The question is, Are you willing to give Him a chance to move in you?

Maybe this has made you think a little about where you stand on the subject. The Holy Spirit is not scary. He is a part of Jesus. He is a part of God. They go together hand in hand. With all three, you have the power to defeat the enemy and stand more firm in the truth of God's Word. The power to resist temptation and sin. The power to stand up for God and not be conformed to the patterns of this world. You have this authority and boldness at your fingertips—you need only ask. Just a thought. Are you walking in authority? Do you want to?

Have I piqued your interest? If so, ask for them, I dare you!

25

SPIRITUAL WARFARE: FIGHT, BATTLE, WAR

*I*AM ECSTATIC THAT you are still here. Anyone who desires more of God will never ever want to go back to what they were before. I am so thrilled. Why? I don't even know you, but you know I prayed over this book for years and for you. And now it is in your hands and you have come all the way. Glory to God.

Guess what? Having discussed the Holy Spirt and His gifts as well as the armor of God, you are ready to talk about the battle.

Let's start with David.

Everyone knows David. He was the boy who killed Goliath with stones and a slingshot. He was the king. He was known as the man after God's own heart. He's a Bible hero. Most men choose him as a favorite, after Jesus, of course. But David did not start out a king with a heart for God. Let's go find David's story in 1 Samuel.

Remember Hannah, the praying momma who wanted a son? She prays and God answers her prayer, and she births, nurses, and weens her son and literally gives him to God. Hannah takes him to the church and leaves him with the priest Eli. He is raised and trained there and is called to be a prophet of God. His name is Samuel. You can read about this story in 1 Samuel 1–4.

During this time, the Israelites wanted a king, so God told Samuel to anoint Saul. This is not the same Saul who becomes

Paul, just to be clear. This is an Old Testament dude who was apparently tall, good-looking, and strong. In 1 Samuel 9:2 God sent Samuel into town and told him whom he was looking for. And God sent Saul into town to find the seer, another name for the prophet. It was a fortuitous moment set up by God. They met, and Samuel anointed Saul as the new king.

Saul did well for a bit and got a little arrogant and snarky and started bucking God and stressing out. Saul sought to find a musician to play for him and calm him down. Enter David.

At this point Saul was disobeying God, and God was looking for a man after his own heart to be king. In 1 Samuel 13:14, God told Samuel to go to the house of Jesse and find the new guy. This story is found in 1 Samuel 16–17. Samuel met all seven of Jesse's sons and didn't get the "This is the one" vibe from God. Samuel was like, "Hey, Jesse, is this all the sons you have?" Jesse said, "Well, my youngest is shepherding the flock." Jesse actually had a son he didn't invite because he didn't think he was the man.

They sent someone out to get David and bring him to the house, and the Lord spoke to Samuel, "Arise, anoint him, for this is he" (1 Sam. 16:12, MEV). Then, the glory fell, y'all; the presence of the Lord came upon David right then. First Samuel 16:13 says, "Samuel took the horn of oil, and anointed him in the midst of his brothers. And the Spirit of the LORD came on David from that day forward" (MEV). Mic drop. So cool.

So let's circle back to teenager David. They had to go to the fields to find him because he was a shepherd boy. We don't find out about David really until he went to take lunch to his three oldest brothers in chapter 17. They all treated him as if he was a kid and asked what he was doing there. He just wanted to give them their lunch and figure out why everyone was letting Goliath the giant talk smack to them. So David said, "I'll go." His brothers and the other soldiers thought, "Yeah, right." Here is what goes down from chapter 17, verses 33–40 (NIV):

> Saul replied, "You are not able to go out against this Philistine and fight him; you are only a young man, and he has been a warrior from his youth." But David said to Saul, "Your servant has been keeping his father's sheep. When a lion or a bear came and carried off a sheep from the flock, I went after it, struck it and rescued the sheep from its mouth. When it turned on me, I seized it by its hair, struck it and killed it. Your servant has killed both the lion and the bear; this uncircumcised Philistine will be like one of them, because he has defied the armies of the living God. The LORD who rescued me from the paw of the lion and the paw of the bear will rescue me from the hand of this Philistine." Saul said to David, "Go, and the LORD be with you." Then Saul dressed David in his own tunic. He put a coat of armor on him and a bronze helmet on his head. David fastened on his sword over the tunic and tried walking around, because he was not used to them. "I cannot go in these," he said to Saul, "because I am not used to them." So he took them off. Then he took his staff in his hand, chose five smooth stones from the stream, put them in the pouch of his shepherd's bag and, with his sling in his hand, approached the Philistine.

During his time in the wilderness shepherding his father's sheep, David was alone. He was out there working in nature, and you know what happened? He discovered who God is, and he discovered who he is. He spent time learning to praise the Lord with his music. Romans 1:19–20 (MEV) says:

> For what may be known about God is clear to them since God has shown it to them. The invisible things about Him—His eternal power and deity—have been clearly

seen since the creation of the world and are understood by the things that are made, so that they are without excuse.

David discovered the heart of God while he was in nature learning to survive, learning to pray, learning about and hearing God, learning who God is. In this he discovered who he is. This time was the beginning of when David developed what God knew He needed in a new king, a man who would serve God well and become a man after God's own heart.

This young teen knew God well. This is why he was able to respond to the soldiers the way he did in 1 Samuel 17:26: "What will be done for the man that kills this Philistine and takes away this reproach from Israel? For who is this uncircumcised Philistine that he should defy the armies of the living God?"

David couldn't believe the soldiers had stood there for forty days listening to Goliath rebuke Israel over and over and do nothing. He came in from the wilderness and getting to know God and thought, "What is happening? Why would you allow this guy to talk about God and our nation this way? Aren't you guys going to do something about this guy and his mouth?"

Next, David learned how to protect, defend, and fight while he was out on the land. In Verses 34–35 he talks about the lion and bear he defeated. David tells Saul, "When a lion or a bear came and took a lamb out of the flock, I went out after it and struck it, and delivered the lamb from its mouth; and when it arose against me, I caught it by its beard, and struck and killed it. Your servant slew both the lion and the bear."

Every time David saved a lamb from death, he learned how to protect, defend, and fight. Each battle grew David inside and out. Each fight taught him how to battle, deeply enough that when he saw Goliath, he just saw a man who was ridiculing his God. God had nestled a place inside the heart of young David. From that place came a deep love for God and a boy willing to defend his God.

This developing deep heart for God brought on these words next, from verses 36–37 (MEV): "This uncircumcised Philistine will be as one of them, because he has reviled the armies of the living God.... The LORD who delivered me out of the paw of the lion and out of the paw of the bear, He will deliver me out of the hand of this Philistine."

David had no doubt God would rescue him from Goliath. He was sick of listening to Goliath trash God. He was confident in himself and with God's hand over his life, and he knew he could win. Why? Every battle had been building the warrior in David.

David took off the armor, went to the brook and grabbed five stones, took his staff and his sling, and went to battle. Goliath mocked David, and David responded in verses 45–46: "You come to me with sword, a spear, and a shield, but I come to you in the name of the LORD of Hosts, the God of the armies of Israel, whom you have reviled. This day will the LORD deliver you into my hand. And I will strike you down and cut off your head" (MEV). Then, David said, "It is not by sword and spear that the LORD saves. For the battle belongs to the LORD, and He will give you into our hands" (v. 47, MEV).

David declared the battle belongs to the Lord. He said *our* hands, not my hands. Maybe he meant the entire army, but maybe he meant his and the Lord's, because David knew his victory would come because he knew his God. He also knew the battle was the Lord's. He fought for God, not for man. He fought a giant because the giant cursed his God. He wasn't having it. He fought for, with, and unto the Lord.

This battle with Goliath wasn't David's first battle, and it sure wouldn't be his last. He would lead armies into battle, love and lose loved ones, make massive mistakes, dance before the Lord, and much more. His life would not be easy; it would be very hard. Every battle would create a deeper love in his heart for the Lord. Every battle would be a war. He would suffer in the physical, mental, emotional, and familial areas of life. But he would also battle in his mind and in the spiritual realm. He was about to embark on some serious spiritual warfare.

The whole reason I went into the detail I did about David is that we can learn a lot from him. Spiritual warfare is very real. It can be hard to understand and even recognize.

The very first thing the enemy does is keep you busy and throw everything at you to keep you from the Word of God. Why does He care? Spending time in the Bible, reading, digging in, and beginning to understand the Word of God makes you stronger. The wisdom that comes from hiding God's Word in your heart begins to create in you a heart after God.

The more time we spend in the Bible, the more we hear God speak. We learn to receive the Word of God as truth. The Bible is God's own words, already anointed by God himself, ready to be used to fight the devil and his minions.

Second Timothy 3:16–17 says, "All Scripture is inspired by God [God-breathed] and is profitable for teaching, for reproof, for correction, and for instruction in righteousness, that the man of God may be complete, thoroughly equipped for every good work" (MEV).

Reading the Word of God helps you get to know God more and equips you. It teaches you and trains you in righteousness. It prepares you for battle.

Hebrews 4:12 says, "For the word of God is alive, and active, and sharper than any two-edged sword, piercing even to the division of soul and spirit, of joints and marrow, and able to judge the thoughts and intents of the heart" (MEV).

Not only does it teach us; it digs in deep into the guts of

us and works on us intricately. It even separates our thoughts and intentions and motives. God's Word is powerful. You get in it; it will change you—for the better. You will find God there. You will find His love, and you will find who you are.

I can tell you right now, you are a warrior. You may not see it yet, but you are. You were made to battle. Every hard thing you have gone through that did not kill you actually made you stronger. Warriors aren't bought; they are built.

In what way are you like David?

Have you been rejected by your friends or family and told you weren't good enough?

Have you been left alone to find yourself in the midst of the noise? Or was it in the silence?

Have you fought someone bigger than you and lost? Did you actually lose, or did you come out on the other side different and better?

See, you are a warrior.

What does that mean? How do you realize your warrior potential? Let's personalize this. How do I see myself? Could I really be a warrior? What does God see in me?

Really ask yourself these questions. Sit in the quiet and listen. He is always speaking; you just have to shut off the noise around you. Remember, He is in the whisper, not the lightning.

When I first learned to do quiet times, I would sit and ask God some really weird questions. What is Your favorite color? What flower do You like best? What flower do You see when You see me? What tool in a toolbox do You see in me? Why?

Weird, right? The reason I did it this way is so I knew when I "heard" Him, it wasn't me talking. As I grew my ears to hear His voice, I was also reading the Bible more and praying more. I began to love spending time with God. I would get excited to get up and hang out. He started waking me up with a song in my heart He wanted to hear me sing in my worship time. Y'all, I am not the greatest singer, but God did not care; He just loves my worship of Him.

I used to read the Bible and fall asleep. Then it started becoming interesting and making sense. I could actually apply these stories to my own life. I started praying small, then started praying God's promises to remind Him, and I was reminding myself. I eventually started believing all of them and seeing Him move in my life. I started praying for healing for my kids and asking for the gifts of the Holy Spirit, and He showed up. He started giving me the Holy Spirit, and I started to walk in His authority.

Boy, did my boldness and prayers change then. All it took was time and faith. It doesn't have to be hours with Him. It doesn't even have to take years to grow in your faith and gifts. It just takes you starting.

In all the time I was doing this, God was equipping me as we discussed. He was training me in righteousness—not my righteousness but His. He was helping me understand Him and love Him more. In doing that, I started to love His people more. My prayers became louder and bolder, meaning I didn't hide in my closet to pray. I started praying for my friends over the phone and praying for my kids out loud, sometimes even in my prayer language. I didn't want to hide anymore because I had fallen so in love with Jesus I wanted everyone to know Him and love Him as I did.

My husband even said to me once, "I think you love Jesus more than you do me." I told him he was right. I did. And that love for Jesus would be what kept us married and made me grow to love him more and better. I needed to know the heart of Jesus to love my husband well, and also to raise my boys to love God and lead them to Him. So as I grew in the Lord, He helped me train our sons. As we raised our sons, we had fights.

The fights prepared us for the battles, and the battles prepared us for the war.

God made me a prayer warrior because He knew the enemy wanted my marriage and my family. He grew me in His Word and in trust of Him because He knew I would have to war for my children's souls. He knew the enemy would come hard and fast and I would be blindsided.

Well, he did. And I was.

If I hadn't spent time with the Father and learned to trust Him, we never would have made it. I had to learn to battle. I had to go deeper in prayer and learn to trust God. I had to relinquish control and let Him have them. Life is spiritual warfare. This world is wicked and mean. Satan wants your marriage and your children. It is up to you to not let him win.

Satan wants them sick. So we pray for healing and declare boldly by His stripes they are healed. And we pray again and again, until God wins and you see healing. Even if it's seven days later and the flu ran its course. You keep praying and touching them and proclaiming life and health and wholeness. You proclaim the Word of God over your children, and while you pray it, they take it in their ears and hear you speaking God's Word because you took the time to hide it in your heart. Why? So when the battle comes, you have the weapon of the Lord in your hand, the sword of the Spirit, the Word of God.

If they are in an accident or the hospital, you play worship music in the room, and you gather around and touch your child or spouse and pray out loud if you have to and bring heaven down into that room. You declare with faith what God's Word says about being healed, living and not dying, and declaring the works of the Lord (Ps. 118:17). You pray in your prayer language if you have it and plead with the Holy Spirit and the Spirit of God for your family.

First Corinthians 14:14 says, "If I pray in an unknown

tongue, my spirit prays, but my understanding is unfruitful. What is it then? I will pray with the spirit, and I will pray with the understanding. I will sing with the spirit, and I will sing with the understanding" (MEV).

When you pray in the Spirit, you are praying with the Holy Spirit in words you don't understand, a heavenly language. When we are in desperation and don't know what to say, the Spirit speaks for us. The Holy Spirit understands the will of God.

Romans 8:26–27 explains this: "In the same way, the Spirit helps us in our weakness. We do not know what we ought to pray for, but the Spirit himself intercedes for us through word-less groans. And he who searches our hearts knows the mind of the Spirit, because the Spirit intercedes for God's people in accordance with the will of God" (NIV).

When we pray in the spirit, we are praying with the Holy Spirit, who knows God's good, pleasing, and perfect will (Rom. 12:2). Who better to pray for your family than the Holy Spirit Himself!

When you come to the end of yourself and you don't know what else to do, you pray.

Two of my three sons had asthma when they were younger. One of them ended up at the children's hospital with pneumonia after an unexpected ambulance ride because he was worse than we thought. He was nine years old. I was so worried. They ran all kinds of tests and poked and prodded, and he was hooked to lines, but God. All I did was worry, then pray. Pray, then worry, and pray again. Worry doesn't get it done, but prayer does. Once he was better, we went downstairs and saw the children who basically lived in the hospital, with way worse issues than I had ever walked through. It put life back into perspective. His situation may not have been as dire or lifelong, but it was big for us. Because it was big for us, it was big for God. We prayed, and He moved. That's just the way my God works.

About ten years later, one of the boys was in an automobile accident. He came in late and didn't tell us until the next morning. He could have broken his ribs or back or even died from internal bleeding. Thank God he didn't. He came in to tell us and was covered in road rash and bruises. I was scared, and my mind went wild. I had to chill and give him to God. All we could do was pray. From the looks of it, I knew it could be bad. God spared him because He wasn't done with him. He still has a purpose and plan for him. Pray is all you can do when you don't know what else to do.

When your kids are small, you lie awake checking temperatures, making sure they are breathing and comfortable. The exhaustion of caring for a sick kid is usually what makes the caretaker sick afterward. The worry, the prayer, the checking on and not sleeping. That is the story of a young parent. When your kids start dating, head to college, or move out, the sleepless nights change. Now you pray in their rooms and beg God to keep reminding them who they are and whose they are. You pray they stay pure from sex, drugs, and all the rest. You pray they find a church and good friends. You pray they call home and come home.

When they are older, if they are not following the Lord or are trying out the ways of the world, the real battle begins. All the sleepless nights, the praying in their rooms—those times accumulate for the real war. The real war comes when the enemy comes for your marriage or your kid. No matter what age they are, they will always be your child. You will always be their parent, and you will be the one who has the most authority, given by God, to pray for them and defeat Satan. You put in the time before so when he comes hard and fast, you are ready for the war.

The enemy will try to tell you it is not working. You may be given dreams and visions of what is going on. You may even get sick to your stomach when you are supposed to pray for them. God knows; listen to the still, small voice. Trust your intuition because when you are in tune with the Holy Spirit, it is usually not wrong. If you get woken up in the middle of the night with a dream of your child and demonic oppression, stop and pray. Intercede for your children, marriage, and family. Pray until the pressure goes. (Check the chapter on intercessory prayer for reminders.)

Whether your children are little or big, it is never too late to start praying for them. Give yourself grace if you are just starting. God is a big God, and He can cover all the years in an instant. Pray for your spouse too. They can always use it. You will see transformations in yourself and them. Pray for your parents and siblings, even if you are estranged or mad at them. Prayer and forgiveness are the best healers. Pray for your children's spouses and families. It is never too late for that either. I started when I had all sons because I knew I would only have "daughters" who loved me if I covered them now and believed God big for them. Just pray. If you don't know how, just talk. He's always listening.

Some of the best books I have found for battle prayers are the books by Stormie Omartian. I have three I use daily and have tabs in them to go straight to a prayer. The prayers are powerful and get the job done. When in doubt, pray the prayers in these books, and the Lord will remind you more to pray to personalize it to your child, spouse, or friends. I own *The Power of a Praying Wife*, *The Power of a Praying Parent*, and *The Power of Praying for your Adult Children*. Each chapter is full of good stuff that teaches you about prayer and then a prayer at the end of each chapter. It is a great start and a great go-to source.

When you don't know what to do, it is nice to have a go-to. I heard a friend say, "Go to the throne before you go to the phone." Go to God first. Pray about it first. Sometimes He answers immediately, and you won't have to phone a friend. Go to the throne first. Go boldly, as the Bible says: "Let us therefore come boldly to the throne of grace, that we may obtain mercy and find grace to help in time of need" (Heb. 4:16).

It is a blessing to have praying friends. I do, and they are game changers. When you have people to stand in the gap and hold your arms up like Moses' friends, it is so powerful. They pray for you and your kids as if they are their own. These kinds of friends are few and far between, but they are out there— ask God for them, and He will bring them. The point is to have trusted voices and confidants,

WHEN WE PRAY, LIVES CHANGE, PEOPLE ARE HEALED, STRONGHOLDS ARE BROKEN, SICKNESS HAS TO FLEE, MINDS ARE CHANGED, HEARTS ARE MENDED.

but they don't have to know everything. You have Jesus as a best friend, and there is no one better. Learn how to trust Him first; then, when you cannot do it alone, phone a friend and get support. A good support system invades heaven and fills the bowls of heaven.

In fact, Revelation talks about these bowls each of the twenty-four elders carry in heaven. When they take the scroll to the Lamb of God for Him to open, the elders have the golden bowls. Revelation 5:8 says, "each one having a harp, and golden bowls full of incense, which are the prayers of saints" (MEV). The prayers are collected in heaven in bowls made of gold. Each prayer is important to the Lamb of God. He hears each prayer we pray, each prayer our friends pray, and each prayer prayed throughout the generations for you and yours. What a mighty, awesome, and loving God we serve.

When we pray, lives change, people are healed, strongholds

are broken, sickness has to flee, minds are changed, hearts are mended. God hears and cares about every single prayer. Not only that, but when we pray, we grow. Our faith grows, our trust in God grows, and our belief that He is who He says He is and will do what He says He will do grows. Prayer is one of the most important things you can do in your life. It increases your faith, hope, and love. Prayer moves mountains and sets you free.

"Where the Spirit of the Lord is, there is freedom" (2 Cor. 3:17, NIV).

Do your time with the Lord, and make prayer a lifestyle. If you don't have anything major happening right now, store up the prayers in heaven for when you do, because the time will come when you will want to know you can trust God to answer your prayers. All the times you pray about the little things are the little fights you cut your teeth on. When the fights get bigger, they become battles. You have to win some small fights to keep from shying away from the harder ones that cause you to battle on your knees in prayer. There will be times when only God can fix this one.

I have mentioned some of the ways that I battle, but let me give you a few ideas of how this works so you can try it, pray about it, or disregard.

ANOINT AND PRAY OVER THE ROOMS OF YOUR HOME

Many years ago I started praying in my kids' rooms. It started at their beds when they were going to sleep, then when they were sick. As I would sit by them and pray, I realized I had kingdom authority as their mother. Remember how I said I would ask my mom to pray and then to call my Big Pop. By the time I had toddlers, I had realized I could reach God too.

When I began to see things like arguing, division, and

attitudes, I decided to start praying over their rooms. I grabbed my oil and anointed the doors as the Israelites did during the plagues in Exodus 7–12. The Israelites anointed their door-posts with the blood of a lamb to keep the spirit of death from coming in their houses. We can do that. Now, don't go killing a lamb; any kitchen oil works. Oil was used in the Bible to anoint the priests and kings. Or you can just touch the door-post as a symbolic gesture.

Touch the doors and begin to pray for angels of protection to surround your child, your home, and their room, including their dreams and social media and friendships. Ask the Lord to defend your home against the enemy and his lying spirits. If you give it a minute, the Holy Spirit may nudge you as to which spirit is trying to interfere with your child. Pray in the room and ask the Holy Spirit to show you if there is anything evil in the room or that your child is involved in. Evil can come in through any open door—television, music, social media, friendships, and so on. Be ready to break the access of that spirit over your child and your home.

Pray for their heart, their friendships, their relationship with you and their siblings, their desire and heart for God. Once you get going, the Holy Spirit will just bring words to your mouth, and Scripture will come out. When you have done the time to pray and hide His Word, these moments are so full of spiritual authority you will be blown away at the power.

PRAYER-WALK YOUR HOME, PROPERTY, AND ROOMS

Similar to anointing the room, you can do this over your entire home. Anoint all entry doors; walk to the corners of the house or property and pray. Some people set up rocks as foundation stones. Jesus told Simon Peter in Matthew 16, "Upon this rock

I will build my church; and the gates of hell shall not prevail against it" (KJV). Your home *is* your church. Your family is the body of Christ. You and your spouse are the pastors and shepherds who lead the sheep, your children. Your home can be built upon the rock of Jesus. You can set up boundaries and rules, just as God did with His church. The rocks are also symbolism of building your house upon Jesus as your rock. Declare that hell and Satan's demons cannot come inside or near you and your kids. If you are inside, open the door and kick Satan out. Don't be ashamed or embarrassed to do this. Who cares what anyone thinks; this is a life-or-death situation here. You are covering and defending your family. This is war. You can do this. You can pray circles around your home and your kids. Ask for protection and angels. Cover them in prayer. Get busy kicking butt and taking names. Their lives depend on it.

HIDING GOD'S WORD IN YOUR HEART

Psalm 119:11 says, "I have hidden your word in my heart that I might not sin against you" (NIV).

When you hide God's Word, not only does it keep you from sinning against God; it arms you with ammunition against the devil. Memorizing Scripture can be fun and can be made into a game. We use note cards. We tape them up on the mirror of the bathrooms. Have your kids pick a verse and write it on a note card or use a dry erase marker and draw it cute on the mirror. All of you memorize together. Start with the one I just mentioned, and explain to the kids why it's important to hide His Word. Or start with John 3:16. Whoever memorizes gets to go get ice cream on Friday night. Make it fun, not a chore. If you have competitive kids, make it worth their time.

Another thing you can do is write verses on note cards and

pray them over your children and spouse. Just put their names in there, like this one in Romans 12:2:

"Lord, I pray that [INSERT NAME] will not be con-
formed to the patterns of this world, but (s)he will
be transformed by the renewing of their mind, that
You may prove what is the good and acceptable
and perfect will of God for [INSERT NAME] life."

Pick a verse, and insert their name. You can also pray the verses over them and put the note cards under their mattresses, and they will be sleeping on the Word of God and His promises for them. Talk about bringing peace into a place—this will do it.

LAYING IT DOWN

This one is basically symbolic. We take our requests and we lay them down at the feet of Jesus. We can write it all down and lay it on the floor and pray for God to take it. We can write the words and names of the struggles on our hands and lay them at Jesus' feet. Whether you bow or lay flat out, prostrate before the Lord, lay it down. Or you can raise your hands up to heaven with all the things written on your palms or a piece of paper and give it to God. We have a tendency of praying and giving it to God, then picking it right back up. This is a symbolic way you leave it there. I write on my hands, pray fervently, cry some, beg a little, worship God, trust Him, and get back up. Then I wash my hands and face and move on. It is so freeing. The troubles don't disappear, but the weight of them lessens when you pass them to the Father.

Some other easy ideas are to play worship music in the house or let your family hear you pray, even if just at a meal. Well, start there, but grow in it. Ask the kids to pray, and teach them to not be afraid to pray out loud. Let your family see you read your Bible. Talk to them about what you read. Help them to see the Bible is the most beautiful book in the world and has all they need to know inside. Draw them near to God by making God a part of your daily life.

Life will be hard, and you will get through everything it throws at you. But it sure is easier when the storms come to fully rely on God and take the battle to Him. He is ready and willing to draw swords and fight alongside you. Zechariah 4:6 says, "'Not by might nor by power, but by My Spirit,' says the LORD." Do not battle alone; let go of the control and give it to the Lord.

Each of the fights prepares you for the battle. They create in you a fierceness that will shine when you are without words, unable to speak or move, have no control over the situation and can only rely on God. These times are the wars. War requires a warrior. A prayer warrior who believes God. A warrior who knows God and what His Word says and stands on it even when you see nothing changing. A prayer warrior who isn't afraid to anoint every room of the house, open the doors and kick out the devil. A warrior who puts on the full armor of God and stands firm in the face of adversity, sin, death, and hell on earth. A soldier who has been built in the battles and bought at a high price by their Savior. This warrior will not back down. This warrior will hold Satan's neck down with his shoe and say, "Nope, not today, Satan. You will not touch my family. You have no authority over me because I am a child of God. You will not win, and you will not take my family."

This warrior pulls a David and says, "You come to me with a sword, with a spear, and with a javelin. But I come to you in the name of the LORD of hosts, the God of the armies of Israel, whom you have defied" (1 Sam. 17:45).

"Be sober, be watchful: your adversary the devil, as a roaring lion, walketh about, seeking whom he may devour" (1 Pet. 5:8, ASV). I am *not* a "whom he may." I am a "chosen people, a royal priesthood, a holy nation, God's special possession, that [declares] the praises of him who called [me] out of darkness into his wonderful light" (1 Pet. 2:9).

My friend, it is never ever too late to start any of this. Do not tell yourself you have failed if you have never done this. That is a lie from the enemy to take you down before you start. Satan knows if you do this, it will change the trajectory of your family. So start. Do not delay another minute. Anything you do is better than nothing. You have what it takes because you have Jesus. Get your praying hands ready.

Today is the day. Yell it if you have to. "Get behind me, Satan! Nope, not today! You are a defeated foe, and you can go back to hell where you belong! Jesus said it is finished and the cross is the final word. So you are done. The end." And that's all, folks.

CHARGE

Fellow prayer warrior, never forget how loved you are. A holy Savior paid the ultimate price for your freedom. Seek His face; dig into His Word. Hide in His presence, and find Him there. Discover the mysteries of His goodness, and let Him reveal who He is and who you are. The victory is yours when the battle is the Lord's. Armor up and stand firm; the enemy won't quit, so neither can you. When the fight comes, be battle ready. War on, Mighty Warrior.

ENDNOTES

CHAPTER 4

1.   Robert W. Bertram, "'Scripture and Tradition' in the Lutheran Confessions," Pro Ecclesia: A Journal of Catholic and Evangelical Theology 10, no. 2 (May 2001), https://doi.org/10.1177/106385120101000204.

2.   "Legalism," World History Encyclopedia, accessed October 18, 2024, Worldhistory.org/legalism.

CHAPTER 7

1.   Girls with Swords Study, Messenger International, accessed October 18, 2024, https://store.messengerinternational.org/products/girls-with-swords-curriculum.

CHAPTER 11

1.   *Merriam-Webster*, s.v. "apostle," accessed October 18, 2024, https://www.merriam-webster.com/dictionary/apostle.

CHAPTER 12

1.   *Oxford Dictionaries*, s.v. "humble," accessed October 18, 2024, https://languages.oup.com/google-dictionary-en/.

CHAPTER 17

1.   Google's English dictionary, Oxford Languages, s.v. "trust," accessed October 20, 2024, https://www.google.com/search?sxsrf=ALeKk03mHFyEmAh3aaMH3jjlr8f5JPnNvg%3A1588280290197&ei=4jurXqvIC4PcswWd6ImQCg&q=define+trust&oq=define+trust&gs.

CHAPTER 19

1.   "Mark Twain Quotes About Loss," AZ Quotes, accessed October 22, 2024, https://www.azquotes.com/author/14883-Mark_Twain/tag/loss#google_vignette.